# A Lightning Bolt of Laughter

by Paul W. Tastad

*Paul Tastad*

**DORRANCE**
PUBLISHING CO
EST. 1920
PITTSBURGH, PENNSYLVANIA 15238

Dorrance Publishing Co
585 Alpha Drive
Suite 103
Pittsburgh, PA 15238
Visit our website at *www.dorrancebookstore.com*

ISBN: 978-1-4809-9157-6
eISBN: 978-1-4809-9371-6

# Children

A Chinese boy had a made in America shirt on. He wanted everyone to know that he was born in America.

The bug man wants his child
to be as busy as a bee
to be as hard working as an ant
to be able to spin a good story as a spider
to be as musical as a cricket
to be able to hop around as needed like a grasshopper
to be as snug in bed as a bed bug

Science treats children like they are some type of experiment. When things go wrong they say it is a chemical imbalance.

The math teacher has a problem child.

A banker said he is disappointed that his son is not going to amount to anything.

A boxer tells his son he needs to knuckle down and get his homework done.

Shoe stores sell lots of sneakers to teachers and mothers so they can sneak up on their kids.

A younger brother runs into the room and hides behind his mother. He said his older brother is after him. The older brother comes into the room covered with paint. Mom asks what happened. The older brother says that he didn't know that when the younger brother wanted to paint him he meant literally.

A child whose dad is a carpenter says all his dad wants to talk about is nuts and bolts.

It isn't so bad that my son thinks he knows everything but that he doesn't think I know anything.

My son is such a dreamer. The other lady says that sounds good. Everyone needs to have dreams. What I mean is that he sleeps all the time.

Dad was happy when the children were old enough so he could read them a bedtime story. He thought now I can find out how the stories ended up that he fell asleep halfway through when he was a child.

The parents were really into reading. They named their daughter paige.

What do you call a father who has been fired from his job? A stay at home dad.

Often when children act up they will look to see if their parents are impressed with their performance.

Father says to his son who is holding a basketball. The ball and you are both full of hot air and you both have a greatly inflated head.

The older brother complains that his younger brother keeps following him. His Mother said "You are a born leader."

A child's dentist said he learned to wrestle on the job. He has had to wrestle many a child to et them in the dentist's chair.

The mother looking at her three wild children who had been giving her problems all day, said it is time to put my problems to bed.

An older man was out with his two daughters. He lives alone. They are always trying to boss him and take care of him. He resents being treated like a child. When they leave the cafe to go across the street, he tells them I don't need your help to walk to the car. I am capable of taking care of myself. He steps off the curb into the path of a car and gets run over.

Boy at his dad's office when the dad's boss enters the room. The boy looked him over and said to his dad, "His head doesn't look too big to me."

A father was listening to his daughter play the piano. She made so many mistakes. The father said that if we were on that old game show name that tune, I don't think anyone would guess what you were playing.

Son says to his dad who is a pastor, after hearing him preach on being a blessings to others, says you can bless me by giving me a raise on my allowance.

My parents don't think I do anything without their nagging me over and over again. I decided to do something out of the ordinary and surprise them. I went outside to wash the family car. I didn't know they would make such a big production out of it. They went outside and sat on two lawn chairs. Soon they were taking pictures of me washing the car and sending E'mails to everyone. Fortunately for me I don't get the energy or idea to surprise them that often.

Your dad expects you to run the business and not run it into the ground.

The parents were busy working the day grandpa came to visit. They asked their teenage son to show him around.
Later they asked him what they did. He said he showed him the museum. He thought they might want to hang around some other older people.

A small boy asks his mother if he can take his stick to bed with him. She asks why. Mom he says it is a night stick.
Table talk for a family with teenagers
Pass the salt
The mashed potatoes are lumpy.
Do we have to eat the peas, I hate peas.
Do you have to make so much noise when your eating?
Can I leave the table now, I need to make a call?
I decided to let them dish up and go watch television.

Learning to enjoy the journey on a trip with three small children.
No matter what I give them they argue and fight over everything.
One gets car sick and has to be by the door. We haven't always made it to a stop either.
Than their drinks, no matter what we usually have something spills.
Than there are the countless bathroom breaks.
I end up taking the wrong turn at least twice.
I argue with my wife about the best way to get there. She thinks she knows more than I do.
Finally an hour before we stop at a motel everyone but the driver is sleeping.
So that night they are all wound up and I can't sleep.
My enjoyment level is not high on these trips.

When roles are played in the home why does the teenage girl usually get to play the role of the victim?

A young boy going with his dad to the shooting range came back tired. He said he was overshot.

A mother says when her children were small they gave her so much love. Now they are teenagers and she says they give her so many headaches.

What most children want to do is to butt in line.

A seamstress is so proud of her son's achievements she can burst her buttons.

A new baby boy was born. The relatives were all looking at him and deciding who he looked like. His little brother said he looks like dad. They are both bald.

Relatives were visiting at the parent's home. Mother started to make dinner. The aunt commented that something sure smelled good. The son said don't be fooled it smells a lot better than it tastes.

Two brothers are in a neighbor's garden pulling up vegetables to eat. The oldest is in middle school while the other one is a few years younger. They had the vegetables in their hands when they heard the neighbor's door open. They dropped the vegetables and started to take off. He yelled at them to stop. He asked them what they were doing. The older boy said we were just taking a shortcut through your yard. The neighbor said "Don't play dumb with me." The younger boy pulled on the neighbor's shirt and said "Sir, he is not playing, he really is that dumb."

A boy comes home from school and tells his mom that he is an idiot. She says you shouldn't say such a thing. Mom you always say not to believe anything unless it is confirmed by three people. Well today a third person called me an idiot.

The tailor's son is afraid of not fitting into school.

My mother was a fan to Teddy Roosevelt. She would speak softly but carry a big stick.

Brother asked his older brother why he can't be an equal partner. The older brother says well the idea is mine, the capitol is mine, and I am the only one that has any money. The young brother complains that his brother just doesn't want to see him get ahead.

The mother comes into the her little daughter's room. There are papers pasted all over the wall. She said Mommy I am papering the walls.

At age twelve everyone in the family knew she wanted to be an actress. When she would act up and throw a temper tantrum her brother would tell her parents not to worry she is just practicing her acting skills.

A father tells his two teenage children when they get off the cruise ship and land he will give them some money to spend. He added that he didn't want them to spend it foolishly. The daughter asked why is mom the only one that can spend money foolishly?

I wanted a horse but couldn't have one. One day Mom said dad is horse. What is up with that?

The family was getting ready to go to church for All Saint's Day. Mom told Carol to get Billy. Mom he can't go. You do know how far Billy is from being a saint.

The seamstress' daughter won the beauty contest. The word is out that she pulled a few strings for her to win.

A fifth grade boy told his mother that when he was walking home several boys behind him started calling him names. His mother was concerned. She asked what he did. He said it was so bad mom they couldn't even remember my name after we had been together for three weeks in school. I felt sorry for them.

It wasn't easy growing up when your mom was a German cook. She always called me her little dumpling.

Growing up the boy knew that when his mother called him to eat and yelled last call, if he didn't come home she would put the food away. I asked if he went home. No, my mother was a health nut and I hated the food. I would beg a friend if I could eat at their house.

Our daughter is gaining weight and we as parents are to blame. She talks all the time. The only way we can get her to stop is to feed her and tell her not to talk with her mouth full.

My son likes chemistry. He is always trying to blow things up out of proportion.

What potato was named for small children? tator tots.

Mom tells her two boys that there is only one piece of cake left so they have to share it. The younger boy comes to her crying. His brother took the top half.

Son asks dad to tell him about the pool in the office. "Why do you think we have a pool at the office?" "I have heard you talking about the office pool."

They got a puppy. Mom put some papers down for him. Her song asked if he was a pedigree. She said no, why? He already has his papers.

Son complained to his baker dad that he didn't know what he was going to come up with for the science fair. Dad said he would try to whip up something.

The teenage girl whose weekend was with her dad wanted to show up how she knew how to drive. She immediately fastens her seat belt and got her cell phone to talk. Dad asked who taught you how to drive. She said mom.

Parents went out to eat with their two small children. On the way home the little boy said to his sister "We are going to get a dog." "Why would you say that?" "Didn't you hear dad asked for a doggy bag and we don't have a dog?"

A daughter tells her mom that she is going to the zoo with her dad tomorrow. The mother corrects her by saying that dad is taking you to work with him. But mom dad says it is like a circus at his job and he works with a bunch of clowns.

After Sunday school a boy tells his mom we need to see more of dad's family. She asks why. Our teacher says we need to reach the heathen.

Never at a family gathering of parents, aunts, uncles and cousins talk about something dumb that you did. They will entertain themselves the next hour talking about other dumb things you have done in the past.

Brother is hitting his younger brother. Mom asks what's wrong. He said he tried to pin a medal on me. What's wrong with that? I had my shirt off.

Besides a naughty child who is sent to their corner? a boxer

A brother is playing a game with his older brother. He yells mom "Didn't you say we have to take turns?" She answered "Yes." He said to his brother "See it is your turn to lose."

Three brothers agreed to come to their parent's house at three and help them move. One brother called at three and said something came up and he would be a little late. He said they should go ahead and start without him. He turns up three hours later after most of the work is done.

A boy asked his dad who is that Uncle Sam we owe so much money to?

The clock maker's daughter is so beautiful. She is a real clock stopper.

Dad's brother who the family rarely sees shown up one time. The son says to the dad "Dad he is white and you said he was the black sheep of the family."

I blame my dad for the way I turned out. He was to good at giving directions. I think he gave me the wrong directions too many times when I was growing up.

The cattle man says he always tried to steer his children in the right direction.

My dad was the strong and silent type. When I would ask for permission to do something he would just nod his head. All in all he made good use of noggin.

Who says "It's later than you think?" A father calling his teenage daughter who is late in getting home from her date.

A family with two teenagers that often complain about everything were eating out in a small cafe. The waitress was sure they hadn't been there before. She asked how they decided to come here. The one said her dad told them if they eat here they will start to appreciate their mom's cooking.

A carpenter said his son is very level headed.

A brother is working to be a ventriloquist. When the brother and his friend came home mom encouraged them to go to the brother's room and see the dummy he made. When they came back downstairs the boy said his friend wanted to know which one was the dummy.

The cleaner says her son is a well polished young man.

The mother asked her son where his older brother was. He told her that he is down the street fighting with Brian. They started the fight earlier, and you know what you always say that we need to finish what we start.

The child of a music teacher complains. The mother says I have heard that tune from you before. Don't use that tone of voice with me.

Two men in their twenties had to stop by the one guy's parent's house. His folks were home, but they hardly spoke to him. The other guy asked why his parents didn't speak to him. He said they are angry with me because I missed a wedding. Well the other guy said they will get over it. Lots of people miss a relative's or a friend of the family wedding. Just give them time. I was supposed to have a part in the wedding. I was supposed to be the groom.

His sister doesn't work in a cheap dollar store. She works in a five dollar store.

The hog farmer had seven children. The smallest one was referred to as the runt of the litter.

Two brothers all their lives were competing with each and trying to get the best of each other. Even after they were married with children they continued this behavior. They are both invited to a relative's wedding which was a distance away there they would need directions to get there. They were about halfway there reading his wife's directions which she had written down. The brother started to laugh. He said he gave his brother's wife mixed up directions and they would get hopelessly lost. His wife wasn't laughing and even looked a little panicked. She said we have been following the directions that your brother gave me.

My brother has been acting like a baseball player. You mean going to bat for others? No, taking swings at others.

The mother really liked her daughter's boyfriend. The father was very critical of him. He didn't think he was near good enough for his daughter. They went with their daughter and her boyfriend to a very expensive restaurant. When the bill came the boyfriend grabbed it and insisted he pay for the meal. So he gave his credit card to the waiter. Only it wasn't his credit card that paid for the meal but the mother's who had given it to the waiter earlier on a trip to the bathroom. The father was so impressed that the boyfriend would get their dinner. He thought maybe he isn't so bad after all.

Remember those birthday parts when you are still a teenager. Sometimes you would have up to three different parties. Now many years later sometimes you go up to three years without having party or admitting you had a birthday.

Two cousins were in a car accident. The mother had already heard they they weren't hurt too badly, but wanted to know how they were doing, so she called her daughter. The daughter said wasn't in too bad a shape but her cousin was in worse shape. The mother says "Oh please would you quit comparing your bodies and just tell me how you are doing."

I loved to visit my uncle who lives on a hog farm in Iowa.
When we eat he always tells us to go ahead and pig out.
One time he offered a guest pig's feet.
He laughs and tells how the guest hog tailed it out of there.

Whoever said "You have nothing to fear but fear itself" has not meet my stepdad.

An actress with small children when she puts them to bed tells them it is curtains for you.

A man reflects that it is not as easy waiting money when the moneys his hard earned money. When he was a teenager it was easier to waste his dad's money.

A head roll can be useful for you when you hear the same thing over and over, or make the same mistake again and again, or when your children do the same dumb things again.

The weatherman had two sons who he named for weather related things. The one was named Gus for a gust of wind. The other was named Ray for a ray of sunshine. Even the grandfather ended up calling him Sonny.

A boy grew so fast he was called a bean pole. He said he just sprouted up so fast.

The small grandchildren were staying with their mother at their grandparents house. At night the children ran into their mother's bedroom and yelled there is a ghost in the house. They heard moaning and groaning coming from their grandparent's bedroom. When asked about it, grandma said that is just the nightly noise grandpa makes.

A little girl tells dad that she saw mama kissing Santa Claus . Boy was dad upset. He wasn't santa this year.

Grandpa who lived alone was entertaining there other guys telling fish stories. His grandson came in and heard him tell of the big one that got away. He said "Grandpa your not telling that story again of how your fist wife left you?"

The fryer became a daddy. He is now called "The fry daddy."

Wall talking is when you think you are talking to your teenagers but actually you are taking to the wall behind them.

It is not easy for the grandfather. He was to get a cake for his little granddaughter's birthday. She wanted Elsie on the cake. The only Elsie he knows is a cow. So he had a cow put on her cake.

The house of cards family
King is the father
Queen is the mother.
One child is the joker.
Every family has a wild card.
There has to be a Jack in the family.
One is number seven she thinks she is perfect.
The ace gets most things rights and things are easy for her.
Two I know you have heard of the terrible two's.
The house of cards is fragile and can fall down anytime.

Grandma is so into cats. The grandchildren have nicknamed her meow meow.

The rain man said we not only need to teach children to come out of the rain, but to be puddle jumpers.

Early on I knew my son was going to be a railroad man. He liked to make tracks. When he sneezed he went ac choo.

# Doctors

Patient to eye doctor is having trouble with his eyes. The eye doctor says "I will see what eye can do."

Patient comes to eye doctor with cross eyes. The doctor says we will see if we can set them straight. The man was talking to eye doctor telling him he sees spots before his eyes. The doctor asked to see his glasses. The doctor looked at them and cleaned them. He said you need to clean them more often.

The eye doctor was up to his eyebrows in bills.

The man tells the eye doctor he doesn't see dots in front of his eyes, but he sees bills. The eye doctor says we all have blind spots.

Doctor's motto "I hope to find a cure for what is ailing you."

The heart doctor says many people have a bleeding heart for others.

The hand doctor asks the patient when does in feel the pain most often in his hand. He says it hurts the most when I write checks to pay the bills.

There are differences in code words. Down here code blue might mean the patient is in danger of dying, but up North they may just be cold and need a blanket.

The man went to the bone doctor. He said he just felt all broken up.

Paul Bunyon was a very famous folk hero in Minnesota. They said wherever he walked that left a lake. He walked all over Northern Minnesota. What people don't know is that he got sore feet from doing all the walking. He had to go a foot doctor. The sores on his feet to this day are called bunions in his honor.

A doctor tells the patent you can't hurt all over. You have to pinpoint one place. I can't treat all over.

When a foot doctor is working on someone's feet and he gets a phone message, he tells the patient to just hold that toe until I get back. When the worker is upset the foot doctor tells him to just go count your toes. The sign on the foot doctor's office says is "Remember Feet First." The foot doctor says if you are going to learn to swim you have to get your feet wet. When most men get cold feet is when they are going to get married.

The old man was dying. The doctor went to check on him and found dogs in his room. He called the nurse and asked her to explain. She said I knew he didn't have much time left, so I called his son and told him could come and bring some of his best friends.

A dentist said he was having fun. He was just teething.

I told the doctor that it hurts every time I move. He said you need to stand still.

A fireman sees a throat doctor. He says he has a burning sensation in his throat.

The wife asks the doctor "Will these pills he takes help him to get better?" "Probably not, but they will put him to sleep, so maybe if he quits complaining the rest of you can get some rest."

A heart doctor gives thanks with a heartfelt gratitude. The heart doctor says some people are not good at at taking a risk. They are faint of heart. A soap opera by a heart doctor is called "Affairs of the Heart." A heart doctor in love says "Be still my heart." The heart doctor says it is important to get to the heart of the matter. A heart doctor has been accused of pulling a few heart strings.

Foot doctor says marry me and you won't be running around foot loose anymore. The foot doctor says you always need to put your best foot forward. If a foot doctor is in a race it is called a foot race. He has to make sure he tows the mark.

The doctor was going over the results of tests that had earlier been given to the patient. The patient was there with his wife and older daughter. The doctor said looking over the results it looks like you have three or maybe four months at the most to live. They started sobbing and holding hands. It was even emotional for the doctor. The nurse knocks on the door. He talks to her and she hands him some papers which he looks over. He said "Folks if I could have your attention. I want you to think of this as a dress rehearsal. You are the wrong Dwayne Johnson. The papers got mixed up."

Brother in hospital tells his sister that she has taken such good care of him. She is his nurse.

The doctor of internal medicine says the reason so many people have stomach problems is that they do much bellyaching.

The doctor of internal medicine said there are just some things I can't stomach.

There are two big battles fought at most hospitals. They are germ warfare and the battle of the budget.

The doctor works with the very ill patients. When he makes a statement he says "I want to be critically clear."

Doctors and weatherman are both concerned about the temperatures.

Only a bone doctor would say he feels it in his bones.

This was the second time in a year the lady had broken a bone. When she went back to the doctor he told her was was sorry she was having so many bad breaks this year.
A hand doctor said that a particular problem stood out like a sore thumb. He also said we need to focus on the problem at hand. A hand doctor makes decisions by the picking of his thumbs.

The woman had surgery. The next day the husband came back to see how she was doing. She said that it only hurts when she laughs. I don't think your sister likes me because she gave me two joke books.

The only dental plan I have is not to see the dentist that often.

A dentist wanted to go out with a smile. At his funeral everyone noticed how white his teeth were. Many were thinking I wish I had had him for my dentist.

My dentist called and said he wanted to see me. I said do you want to pick the place to eat or should I?

The doctor looked the patient over and told him he didn't look too good. The patient looked at the doctor and said "You don't look too good either.

The husband was having a brain scan done. His wife and brother were in the waiting room. When the doctor came back the brother asked the doctor is they found anything on his brain. The doctor said they didn't find anything. His wife said "I could have told you that."

A bone doctor tells the man that there are no more breaks for him.
He also added I am sorry I can't give you a break on the bill.

What road the hospital wants to put you on is the road to recovery.

A dentist wrote a book called "If the Tooth be Told."

In visiting a mental hospital if one of the patients is talking to himself don't interrupt.
That is considered being rude. At the mental hospital a man is jumping up and down
throwing a temper tantrum. The doctor said not everyone can do that so good.

The foot doctor says that many people are just not sure where or when to put
their foot down. The foot doctor loves it when he teachers and everyone sits at
his feet. When a foot doctor knows something is wrong he says "Something is
afoot." The foot doctor says we have to learn to stand on our own two feet. We
need to be careful not to step on someone's else toes. We needed to start on the
same foot. The foot doctor helps people to get back up on their feet. The feet
are the main part of the body people complain about. They say they have been
on their feet all day. The foot doctor says there has been a problem lately with
bosses keeping the workers on their toes. It isn't good to walk on your toes. He
says when his workers get upset he tells them to count their toes. To get the day
started right he has them touch their toes. It gives them a touchy toe sort of a
feeling. A new book out by the foot doctor is titled "My Ingrown Toe Nail."

Things didn't go well at the mental hospital when a worker asked his boss for
a raise. The boss asked "Are you a lunatic?"

The skin doctor says we need to be comfortable in our own skin.
Some people get into trouble because they show off too much skin. Remember
beauty is only skin deep.

The dentist works in a rough part of the city. He has a sign that says "If you
are going to lie through your teeth make sure they are clean. Lying through
your gums just doesn't have the same effect."

An operating doctor chews out another operating doctor telling him that is not the way we operate around here.

My Uncle is fully committed. It looks like he is going to be in the mental hospital for a long time.

A man asked the doctor to examine his head. The doctor asked why. He said so many people have been telling him that he needs to have his head examined.

It pains me to have to see the doctor.

A nurse with a bad attitude was preparing to give a patient a shot. She said to the other nurse that she was going to stick it to him.

A patient was complaining to his psychologist how all his problems were other people's fault. It was the blame game all over again. Finally the psychologist suggested that maybe there was something he could change about himself. He said I have already tried that. I have been married twice before.

A doctor was stapling lady's stomach together when he ran out of staples. He yelled for the nurse to get the glue gun.

A man at the mental hospital is blessed. He doesn't have to take drugs to see things or have an out of the body experience. He has them anyway.

Many people in the mental hospital have ideas, but remember it is a mental hospital and many of their ideas are crazy. Also we have a lot of retired university professors here that didn't have far to go to be crazy. The number one name the people want to called is professor.

The psychologist said to the patient when I told you to name your problems, I didn't mean for you to give me people's names.

The back doctor had some back issues with the editor.

When nothing bothers a back doctor he says it is no skin off his back.

A big husky guy was getting a shot and some blood work. He kept worrying that it would hurt too much. The nurse said she had never seen anyone making such a fuss. She asked what he did for a living. He said he was a boxer.
The only person you can't fool at a hospital. It is the X-ray technician. He can see right through you.

Riding in the back of an ambulance the man yells "Would you slow down, I don't want to get killed in an accident before we reach the hospital.

Another man riding in an ambulance yelled at the driver "Would you turn the air on, I am dying back here."

The bone doctor has a fractured relationship with his son.

The waiting room at the doctor's office was full. The first one was called back to see the doctor. The doctor had to do some procedures with him that were quite painful. The man yelled "ouch your hurting me." Soon he yelled "Please I can't take anymore." Finally he shouted "No doctor it is too much ow." The doctor is finally done. He tells the nurse to send in the next patient. She says what patients the waiting room is empty.

The counselor said when I wanted you to be open about your feelings with others, I didn't mean about your negative feelings towards them.

A lady asked another lady whose brother was in the hospital was he was doing. She said the doctors said he was stable. The other lady said they better keep him, he hasn't been stable in years.

The counselor asks the patient how he has been doing in handling his guilt feelings. He said so much better. Now when I do something mean to others, it doesn't bother me at all.

# Law/Lawyers

A lawyer gives the defendant a worse case scenario. You go away for 30 years, while with the money I made working on this case I take a much need vacation to the Bahamas.

A policeman admits sometimes he does things a little off the beat.

Police are responding to a burglary at a home. Told the owner to wait in the kitchen until they get there. They noticed where the lock was broken to get in. The owner said a computer and a few other things were taken downstairs. They followed the officer upstairs as they went through each room. The last room was a terrible mess, clothes were thrown all the over, the drawers had all been pulled own and trash was piling up. You could hardly walk in the room. The officer said it looks like the burglar trashed this room. The mom explained that is her teenage son's room and it always looks like that.

In the old days if a detective stepped on gum he was called a gumshoe.

Words in the office of a lawyer most often spoken to the secretary are "make me a copy."

Thief says he doesn't really steal things he just borrows them and forgets to give them back.

Can you get a straight answer from a dishonest crook?

The police picked up a mime for questioning. So far he hasn't said a word.

The defendant does not like the verdict. He says it is mistrial of justice.

A man who worked at a bank had embelized thousands of dollars. He felt they would not find any evidence because everything was shredded. There was not a shred of evidence to be found.

The man was all upset. He was going to shoot himself. Like so many people he ended up shooting himself in the foot.

The lawyer asked the defendant if he knew anything about the missing bonds. He said my mother said there is a time to talk and a time to be silent.

A lawyer during the break had put his case on the judge's bench. The judge came back and looked at the case and asked what it was doing here. The lawyer said "I rest my case."

A detective hurt his foot. He had been working in the evidence room, and he dropped some hard evidence on his foot.

A lawyer asked the defendant if he could remember what he did on the night of the 15th of this month. The defendant thought for awhile and finally said he couldn't remember anything about the evening. A lady stands up in court and yells "You fool. You spent the night with me and said it was a night you would never forget."

Two detectives are questioning a man who the needed to get information from to solve a case. He said his lips are sealed. He promised he would never tell so there is no use asking him anything. The one detective pulls out a fifty dollar bill and shows it to him. The man grab it and says okay now what do you need to know?

Defendant says in court that he should have listened to his wife. She always said never leave fingerprints.

Can crooks make honest mistakes?

The word any criminal hates to hear is "busted."

A lawyer said his former job in construction has helped him in his job. He has learned how to build a case.

A lawyer says to the defendant that if the facts are known we are in big trouble.

One detective tells the other detective investigating the robbery at the store, that the robbers must have been cleaners. The way they cleaned out the safe and didn't leave any footprints or finger prints.

The defendant would not shut up in court. Tired of all the interruptions the judge asked the balilif to bring in a gag. He was issuing a gag order and wanted to gag the defendant.

Two detectives were looking for clues in a a man's apartment. "Sam get out of the refrigerator were looking for clues and not food.

The defendant was asked on the witness stand if he had met to shoot his father-in-law. No sir, that was not my intention. I was aiming for my brother-in-law when my father-in-law got in the way.

A detective says lots of people he talks to clam up.

Lawyers were talking about the bad cases they had in the past. The youngest was too young to have a bad case yet, so he said he had a bad case of the flu not too long ago.

A lawyer says to another lawyer "We would have won the case if the jury only had a little more imagination."

Two groups known in stall tactics are teenagers and lawyers.

The lady was a witness to another lady pushing her boyfriend in front of a car. The lawyer asks her to describe what happened. "I tell you that lady really got herself done up. Her hair looked wonderful. Her makeup couldn't have been better and than her nails. She looked great." I was behind her when she left the salon and a nasty guy was a sneer on his face met her. He didn't even glance at her, but started to talk ugly to her. I thought what a jerk." Now the lawyer asked "Did you see her push him in front of the car?" Well maybe she gave him a little nudge, but he sure had it coming.

The prosecutor tells the witness that he couldn't be further from the truth. The defendant whispers to his lawyer "I could get a lot further from the truth."

Two detectives were looking over a crime scene. The victim was laying face down with a knife in his back. The older detective said we need to figure out what happened here. The younger one said he was on it. It looks like he turned his back on someone he trusted and he stabbed him in the back. We need to look for a back stabber.

A lawyer talking to his daughter about her new boyfriend. Your mom and I haven't reached a verdict on him yet.

A judge likes order. He divorced his wife for disorderly conduct.

A man on the witness stand admits that maybe he was wrong. There are gasps in the audience. The judge says to the recorder make sure you have that statement recorded. The lawyer asks if he could repeat what he said again. This is what happens when you finally admit you did something wrong.

A lady went before the judge to get her name changed to Charity. When asked why, she told him her very rich grandfather was going to leave all his money to Charity.

The client asked his defense lawyer what he thought he should do. The lawyer said the way the case is going and the strong evidence against you, I would hop on a plane and get out of here.

For twenty years the policeman walked the beat in the same neighborhood. Now another policeman is walking the same beat. The beat goes on.

Many witnesses act like older people on the witness stand. They say they can't remember.

A lawyer asked the man on the witness stand what he thought about John Dorian. He said he couldn't answer. His mother taught him that if you can't say anything nice about someone than don't say anything at all.

Send your lawyer a text. It costs too much to talk to him. A lawyer was holding his case and leaning towards that side. He said he had a heavy case load.

The defendant talks all the time. It is difficult to get him to shut up. He takes the witness stand and doesn't have anything to say.

Over the police radio it says attention all units be on the lookout for the cat burglar. I heard she is on the prowl again.

The polite bank robber helped an older woman into the bank by taking her by the arm and saying "May I." What he asked the teller for money he remembered to say "Please." He left by telling her to have a good day.

The police can't find out much information about the man. Another officer said he always kept a low profile.

A lawyer was complaining to a client that everyone think all he wants is there money. I am tired of people thinking I am always finding new ways to charge them. I don't even want your money. Now get out. Oh and would you leave me a check on your way out.

A detective said he was able to solve the problem by connecting all the dots.

The lawyer said he sure wished he could read faces better.

The defendant tells the lawyer the real story of what happened. After listening the lawyer says you are going to have to make up a story. No one is going to believe the story you are telling.

The man was preparing to take the oath "Do you promises to tell the truth." The defense attorney said he objects. This man has been a career politician for the past thirty years. I really doubt that he is able to tell the truth.

A lawyer talking to another lawyer
At home when he says something his wife will say you are overruled.
When he tells his children to do something they say they object.
His wife is making a case for him to take some time off and take them all on a vacation.
He has hardly found time to read his brief notes.
At different times when someone does something he has trouble figuring out who the guilty party is.
The other lawyer says it sounds like you need to lay down the law.

Lawyer tells the defendant when I nod to you turn your head to the jury and give them your sad dog face. We want some sympathy here.

The cat burglar was brought in for questioning but she wouldn't say a word. It seems the cat got her tongue.

He now works in a sandwich place but you can tell he used to be a policeman. The bread is all laid out and he tells his coworker to spread them.

They caught the window bandit. So far he said he was innocent. He felt like he was being framed.

Five different women had been attacked at the mall. They were women their upper forties or fifty. They were not particularly good looking. The man would run to to them grab them give them a kiss and than run away. The police had rounded up some suspects and were sure that one of them was the right guy.

To make it a even five guys in the lineup one very good looking policeman dressed up in scruffy clothes. The women all looked at them closely. They all picked the good looking policeman. They all decided not to press charges. I think they all got a good story out of this.

The witness was riding with the man who had struck another car. He was asked if he noticed anything unusual about his driving that day. No, he was drinking coffee, fooling around trying to get the right radio station and grabbing a bite to eat. I would have to say it was a normal day of driving for him.

A young man was brought into the police station for questioning. Finally the officer said "I know you promised you would not tell on your friend and or say anything that would get him in trouble. I am going to put some names on a paper. You can just use your finger and point to the right one when I ask the questions." This is what is meant by being fingered.

A man was given a ticket for jaywalking. He claimed he didn't do anything wrong. The officer asked if he didn't see the sign that said "Don't Walk?" He said yes, but I wasn't walking, I was running.

A lawyer complained that too many lawyers make the cases too big. There need to be more open and shut cases.

A class at the detectives school is called "Name your Poison."

A farmer was arrested. The police found drugs on him. He said it was planted on him.

Sometimes when people think they have committed the perfect murder, they forget about the body of evidence.

The tow truck driver had just gotten out of the bank. A car races in the parking lot and parks in the handicap space and two guys run into the band. The driver hates it when people park in a handicap place when they are in good health. Just to teacher them a lesson he tows their car away. When the two guys go out after robbing the bank imagine their surprise to find their car gone.

It was a sad day for the clock maker. It looked like he would be facing time in prison.

A judge tells the lawyer who has been objecting and objecting that he getting to be too negative.

The judge tells the witness to stop swearing on the witness stand. The witness said I promised my lawyer if I was up here that I would swear.

The astronomer was a star witness.

The lawyer explained to the man in the the bankruptcy court that he had no money. He said he understood, and that's why he has been using credit cards.

The lawyer is talking to the head of the company in bankruptcy court. I see by your records that you laid off 20 employees last year, but at the same time you gave yourself a 20% bonus. Can you explain? Yes, it was such a depressing year. I felt I had to do something to cheer myself up.

A woman was in bankruptcy court up North in the winter. She came to the witness stand wearing a mink coat. She had a diamond decline on and expensive rings on her fingers. Her shoes cost a fortunate. When the lawyer asked her if she had any idea where all the money had gone to, she said she had no idea what happened to the money.

In bankruptcy court when they are looking at where the money went they have to broke it down.

The first exercise given by the policemen was when they would arrest someone and tell them to spread them.

The man in bankruptcy court said he felt at a total loss.

Sometimes the police talk retail talk. They say they have the goods on someone.

# Marriage

When I speak my piece to my newspaper husband he remarks that is just my opinion. He adds that I should not be so opinionated.

A man divorced twice was getting remarried a third time. I said remember two wrongs don't make a right.

The only exercise my husband gets is when he walks in his sleep, so I just let him walk.

A lady married a werewolf. She says he brings out the beast in her.

The tailor says there were some rough patches in his marriage.

Matt has really blessed me. My wife ran off with him and now my life is so peaceful.

The cleaner told her husband that she really doesn't appreciate it when he talks dirty to her.

A man was complaining to a coworker that he had a sore side. Last night we went out with two other couples. He had told his wife to poke him if he was wrong.

When my husband was young he was a well of information. Now as he has gotten older, I am afraid the well has gone dry.

A druggist said his wife was leaving him. It was a bitter pill for him to swallow.

I only married the magician because he said he could be in two places at the same time.

My wife is an actress. It is difficult to find a place to eat where she hasn't already made a scene at the place.

An astronaut doesn't understand his wife. It is like we came from two different planets.

It was a real eye opener for my husband when the neighbor lady was doing a window dressing.

Just because my husband works at a tire company that doesn't mean he isn't thinking. His wheels are always spinning.

A cave man was the first man to admit his marriage was on the rocks.

The man went to the local pub and asked for a bowl of stew. He said his wife had been fretting and stewing all day.

My husband is a butcher. It is not easy getting used to his cutting remarks. When her husband tries something he says I will take a stab at it.

My wife is not the best cook, but when it comes to meals she offers the guest lots of choices. Do you lasagna, chicken, pot pie, tuna and noodles or a pasta dish? She than gets the requests out of the freezer and microwaves the instant dinners.

Two guys were sitting in chairs across from the kitchen table. The man's wife asked what was gong on. He said don't pay any attention to them. They are just two guys from my job. I promised them they could watch my next fight.

The woman's husband worked in the evidence room at the police station He lost some evidence. His wife said you're the wrong man for the job, you lose stuff all the time at home, and I have to tell you where to find it.

A young couple without much money were talking about getting married. He finally asked her. Should we live with your parents or mine?

I don't think my husband will ever leave me. He has no direction in his life. He has always needed me to map out a plan for his life.

Married to a Werewolf
He was a lone wolf, not like his cousin.
His cousin was always trying to be the leader of the pack.
We would get calls at night complaining about a wolf howling at the full moon, and the it would wake up the neighbors.
Other times I would find chicken bones in the garbage. He admitted they were his. He said he was just out for a midnight snack.
I considered leaving him, but than he told me about how alone he felt and that nobody really understood him.
The next night when he was out howling at the moon, soon a second person was howling that would be me. He is no longer a lone wolf.

My brother and his wife are having trouble losing weight. He calls her cupcake and she call him her honey bun.

A mother tells another mother what a mother hen she is. Her kids go peep peep.

A cave man was out late. When he got home his wife asked where he had been. He said didn't you see the picture I left for you on the cave wall?

Wife said when she first met her husband he had no direction or idea of what he wanted to do with is life. Now I give him lots of directions and ideas about what he needs to do with his life.

A cleaner tells her husband if you think I am going to continue to clean up after you, you better think again.

Many a woman has been called a saint for putting up with a husband most woman would dump.

Husband comes in with the three dogs all out of breath. His wife asked what happened. He said I let the dogs out in the backyard. I didn't know the back gate wasn't closed. Sure enough I found them in the neighbor's garden digging it up. The neighbor came out with a bat and he was swearing as he ran towards us. Dogs I said it is time for a run.

My husband wants me to be a heavenly body. He is always saying to me be an angel and do this or get this for me.

It is difficult to be the wife of a fighter. He comes home all bruised up. She says I suppose you have been in a fight again.

You know your wife is probably not the best cook when the dogs don't beg for food at the table.

A man said his two dogs ate his wife's meatballs and he had to take them to the vet. The vet had to get it out of their stomachs. He asked if I was trying to poison the dogs.

A wife is telling another wife how her husband thinks she is such a great cook. He compliments my cleaning, and says nobody can wash and take care of the clothes like I do. The other wife said so you cook, clean and wash clothes all for the reward of a compliment.

A woman complained that not only is her husband a baby but he acts like he is in his infancy stage.

Middle ages
He was her knight in shinning armor.
She was his tower of strength.

Women were talking about what the husbands miss about retirement.

One says he misses getting up early and going to work. Unfortunately he still gets up early and half the time messes up my day.

The other one says he misses his friends and coworkers from They all said they would call, but so far it hasn't happened.

The third said he misses that the children are grown and have moved away. We have a terrible phone bill. Usually they are busy and don't have the time to talk that he does.

The fourth says unfortunately he misses the toilet more often than not.

When we go out to eat my husband wines while I dine.

Waking my dog or waking my husband I get the same results. They both growl at me.

My husband is so unhandy in everything he fixes. After he works on a small problem it becomes a big problem.

It was getting late at night. A couple had been visiting another couple. The man whispered to his wife "We may have overstayed our welcome." The host couple had both changed into their pajamas.

My husband is a dognapper. He likes to take naps with the dogs.

Three women were describing how their husbands were like a pig.

One says her husband eats like a pig. Food is all over the place and he is stuffing it into his mouth. And yes he likes corn and slop. He makes so much noise when he eats.

The second one says her husband lives like we are in a pig sty.

You should see the bathroom when he is done. It takes an hour to clean it up. The rest of the house is a mess too. Clothes dumped everywhere, dishes left everywhere and papers all over. He never puts anything away.

The third says it is worse for her. She feel like she sleeps with a pig. When he snores it sounds just like a pig grunting.

Than he hogs the blanket and the bed, leaving me very little room to sleep. I seldom get a good night's sleep.

After being married a few years my wife said she wanted to hear the patter of little feet. I went out and bought her a dog.

My husband is having a hard time losing weight. He doesn't like to do anything on an empty stomach.

His wife works in an ice cream shop. She think everything will be better if you just put some whipped cream and a cherry on top.

Husband knows that people have been calling his wife crazy for the way she acts. He told them I am her husband and I am the only one who has the right to call her crazy.

An unfaithful man says he has affairs to attend to.

Her husband is so into guns. He says when he does he wants to go out with a bang.

It was another long and cold Minnesota winter with lots of snow. My wife and I decided to escape the weather and take a four day trip to Mexico. I knew we were in trouble when our luggage was lost. We waited for several hours but they couldn't find it. We took a cab to our hotel. Now remember we had on our heavy winter clothes with no clothes to change into. The humidity was terrible, and we were both sweating and smelling by the time we got to our hotel. Our hotel was on the top floor the fourteenth. My wife said look we can see a long way. Then the downpour came. We soon found that we had a leak in our roof with water dripping in the ceiling. My wife said she was hungry. I thought we would take the elevator down and see about an exchange of rooms and get some food, but the note on the elevator said it was no longer working. My wife was not willing to go down the stairs to get food, so she asked if I could bring her something. When I got downstairs there was no one at the desk. The rain was still pouring down so I just dropped into a little cafe by the hotel and got some food. That was our second mistake. By morning we were both very sick. I am sure it was food poisoning. We didn't feel good the next two days. On the third day we received a call from the airport that they had found our luggage. Did we want to come down and get it. I said no we are leaving tomorrow we will just pick it up then. We had been washing our clothes in a sink in the room. One the last day my wife was busy writing postcards to send telling people of the wonderful time we were having and showing things we never saw. We did want them to be jealous. Oh wonderful Minnesota, snow and cold. I promised myself that I wouldn't complain about it again.

My early bird retired husband wakes up too early on a Saturday morning so he decides to mow the lawn. I get a call from my neighbor who lives on one side of us. She has two small children and she says thanks to your husband now everyone is awake. I wanted them to sleep in. Now everyone is going to be crabby. The neighbor across the street came over and noticed the edger that my husband was using. He said you borrowed that over a year ago and took it back. My husband can't always tell what are flowers or weeds and he mowed over some of my flowers. When he came in I was busy calling a lawn service who we were going to use from now on.

My wife is a judge One morning we were having an argument. She said you know I am right. I wear the robe in the family. Hey I said don't discount me I have my bathrobe on.

At the banquet the man was honored as the salesman of the year. He said he wouldn't be where he was today if it wasn't for the wonderful woman in his life who was always there for him and encouraging him and guiding him. Would my mother stand up and take a bow. Unfortunately his wife was there too and prepared to stand up. There is a good chance there is going to be a fight when he gets home.

My wife works in a blood bank. She takes her job very serious. She is always on the lookout for more blood.

A man said his wife goes to a local doctor. His friend thought he meant loco.

My husband would practice his sermon on me and the kids. He would get so preachy.

My new wife wither two children and all their problems came into my life with a lot of baggage. But I can handle it. I am a baggage handler at the airport.

Finally the baker's wife pregnant. She tells her husband there is a bun in the oven. He goes back to look in the oven.

Jane Doe married John Doe. They wanted to remain anonymous.

My wife is in a dangerous mood when she is in a spending mood. You can see the dollar signs in her eyes.

A husband said he had a hard day on the job. His wife asked if he worked hard. He said no he tried to avoid working and the manager all day, and it wasn't easy.

A bail bonds man says to the troubled lady it you marry me I can bail you out when you get into trouble.

A astronomer promised the lady the moon if she would marry him.

A comedian said if you marry me you will a laugh a minute.

A dishwasher says marry me and I promise you no more dirty dishes.

My husband thinks he is a Viking. He is always going on a raid. I know it is usually to raid the refrigerator.

My husband is a take charge person. I have to remind him that he is a retired general.

They didn't want to pay the final bill for the wedding pictures. He still had quite a few to send to them. He touched them up so they both looked twenty years older.

I have had it with my husband. He is an astronomer and is always wanting me to join him in sleeping under the stars. Than he keeps me awake pointing out the different stars.

Two couples are on a driving trip. It is after lunch. The driver is tired. The other three are all trying to sleep. He needed to talk to stay awake so he told them stories about all the close calls he had while driving on trips. Now suddenly they were wide awake and two of them even offered to drive for him.

His wife a very good cook has left him. He says "I don't know where my next meal will come from." She complains to a friend that he treats her like a meal ticket.

A magician's wife said she was tricked into marrying him.

My wife always dreamed of being famous. Finally I got us a red carpet so she can walk on the red carpet.

I asked the man why he decided to be an astronaut. He said the world wasn't big enough for both him and his wife. So it is goodbye world and hello space. His wife said he has always been kind of spacey, and I have wondered if he isn't from another planet.

My husband is a blackjack dealer who always wants to deal with things later.

My husband is acting more like a dog all the time. When he doesn't like someone I have heard both him and the dog growl.

Wife says it isn't so bad that my husband works for peanuts, but do you know how hard it is to clean up after the peanut shells are left all over?

All day long my husband has been feeling fine. I was getting ready for a garage sale and had been sorting stuff in the attic. I asked my husband to move the boxes to the garage. Suddenly he has an aching back.

My husband has a bad heart and can't handle anything exciting. We eat out in places where the food is really bland.

It is difficult when my wife and her sister get to talking. They always try to see who can get the last word in.

A woman complained that her husband is a bundle of nervous energy. The other lady said don't complain. I wish my husband had some energy.

If a wife really wants to smell good for her husband she needs to be a good cook and baker. He comes home and smells her. Hey you smell like roast beef tonight. Another night he says you smell like you have been baking.

My husband has been learning sign language. A car cut him off and my husband put up his finger. I don't know what the man in the other car thought but he raised his fist at my husband. He probably just misunderstood my husband.

A couple was thinking about different things they had done together and having a good laugh about it. The husband shared about all the fun they had on a camping trip. She said that had to be wife number one or two because it sure wasn't me. I never went on any camping trip. Guess who is sleeping on the couch tonight.

There was a rumor going around about the man's wife being unfaithful to him. No one knew what to believe. They were both church going people and no one wanted to gossip about it. Finally at a church supper he shows up wearing a shirt that says "The rumors are true."

The wife had a big garage sale when her husband had gone on a fishing trip. Later when he came home he complained that a new set of tools that he kept in the garage were missing. He was sure she sold them at the garage sale. She doesn't remember and doesn't think she sold them. He is upset with her all week and keep bringing up to her what a dumb and terrible thing she had done. The next week the neighbor across the street comes over carrying the tools. He says he is sorry that when he had loaned them to him that he had kept them so long.

A husband and wife were having a heated argument. She told him that her mother was coming and going to stay a month. He told not to use those scare tactics with him.

A new wife was slim when they got married. After eating out with friends at work and learning to cook at home after a few years she had gained quite a bit of weight. Her husband was heard talking on the phone to a classmate saying that his wife was a lot more than he thought she would ever be.

My wife is an actress. Every little thing she does she wants applause.

When a lady finds a good man, often her single friends will come by the jewelry store looking for good luck charms to help them find the right one.

A couple is getting ready to go to a party. She pulls a dress out of the closet that he hasn't seen before. He asks her when did she get that dress. Oh she said I have had it for some time, it has just been hanging in the closet. He watches her put it on and says "You may want to take the price tag off."

Husband who is way on a business trip calls his wife. She goes on and on about what a bad day she had. Than she say that she wishes he had been here to enjoy it with her.

My brother has had bad luck with marriages. He has been married three times. It took him longer to get married than the length of time the marriage lasted.

A husband was so upset with his wife. He asked how she could do something so dumb. He said are you nuts. She answered that she probably was a little off or she wouldn't have married him.

My husband makes keys. He is the only one I know that can get keyed up about a job. He doesn't want me to give our spare key to anyone.

A man's wife was let go from her job at the daycare. She just wasn't any good with small talk.

My husband likes our two furry dogs. We live up North where it is cold in the winter. During those months I like to wear my furs in the hopes that my husband will notice me too.

When a couple is married so long they can read each other's minds. The husband says to the wife "I second your thought."

My wife has been quite upset about the world going to the dogs because she is a cat person. She has been hissing about it quite a bit lately. She said it has taken her years to claw her way to the top. I am afraid she is ready for a cat fight.

Why did you decide to be a travel agent? In my family and with my first two husbands, I kept wanting to send them somewhere.

Dad tells mom to be an angel and do this and that. He is always telling her what to do. His son asked why he tells mom to do so many things He said she is trying to earn her wings.

My husband plays ruff when he golfs because that is usually where the ball goes.

They say home is where the heart is. Unfortunately my husband's body may be here but his heart belong to someone else.

My husband has trained the dog to be lazy. I ask the dog if he wants to go for a walk or run with me, and he looks at me like I am crazy. My husband asks the dog if he wants to go for a ride and he is right there.

The couple were getting up in age where he was close to retirement. When he slept at night he could sleep through anything. Unfortunately his wife couldn't and than to top if off he had a bad snoring problem. The wife woke up and decided she wouldn't be abele to sleep anymore in their bedroom so she put on her housecoat, closed the door to their bedroom and decided to sleep in the guest bedroom. Now he had set a box of stuff near the stairs so he wold remember to take it to his office in the morning. She thought of something she wanted to get downstairs before the went back to sleep. Not knowing the box was there she tripped on it and fell down the stairs She couldn't move her legs and all her shouting didn't wake up her husband. She knocked a table over and on that table was her car keys. The garage being full of stuff, the car was parked outside. She pushed the alarm button on the car. Soon the alarm was going off and lights were going on down the street. One person had called the police thinking someone was breaking into a car, while other called the husband's phone. He got up and found his wife downstairs, while the police were pounding on the door. Later he had to get an ambulance to take his wife to the hospital. The whole neighborhood was up watching everything. The next day his neighbor said to him "George this used to be a quiet neighborhood until you moved in."

Three golfers were starting a game. The one asked one what his handicap was. The other golfer said "You haven't met his wife yet."

Husband and wife are in divorce court. The husband says my biggest mistake was in marrying you. She says if I am not mistaken you asked me first to marry you.

Attractive people often marry unattractive people so they don't compete with them for attention.

A welder and his bride got married. In their vows they say weld us together.

A man was telling his friend that his wife is always complaining that he doesn't help like he should around the house while she slaves away in the kitchen. His friend said maybe she is right. Please all she does is put an instant dinner in the microwave.

A wife said her husband has been putting so many things behind him. Unfortunately that is giving him a big behind.

I hate it when my wife says I have to suit up.

The water man says his wife can be shallow and such a big drip.

When a couple goes out with another couple the husband always talks about dates when things happened. He gives statistics and lot of facts. Everyone knows he is wrong half the time. His wife is quiet. She never corrects him, but just smiles at him. Now which one is the smartest?

My wife has worked too long in sales and when you try to make a deal with her she makes for a tough bargain.

A card player's wife said she felt like she had a hard hand to play.

Wife talked the husband into getting tickets for a concert and tonight was the night they were getting dressed to go. Like a normal husband he hated to all dressed and go out when he didn't want to. The wife tells him to change the sport jacket he was putting on because it doesn't go with the pants. They get caught in traffic and it takes a good hour to get there. The parking garage is full and they have to find a place to park on the street and than walk three blocks to the theater. Finally they are at the door and he reaches for the tickets. There not there, but in the sport jacket he was going to wear that he left on the bed. This should be an opps moment when we laugh at what happened. But being his wife knew he didn't want to come it wasn't an opps moment for her.

A couple had been visiting the wife's brother. The wife said he is such a character. The husband said yes, he reminds me of goofy.

An appliance salesman was giving a talk on his fifty wedding anniversary. He said you want a solid one. It needs to be well built. It needs stop last through years of wear and tare. It needs to be long lasting. The warranty is sort of like a marriage license. It shows you believe in the product. Now days getting a good appliance that has these qualities or finding a wife with the same qualities is getting hard to find.

The women were discussing Karen's husband. I think he has a drinking problem. When I asked Karen about it she just said he is on a liquid diet.

It can be confusing for many men. With all the dyed hair, the make up and even face lifts among the things it can be difficult to figure out who is the real thing. The one man said he picked the plain one because than he knew what he was getting.

A man is married to Hope. When he wakes up in the morning he wakes up to Hope.

The wife of the railroad worker was rail thin.

They called him Joe Banana because of his banana nose. The last I heard he was splitting from his wife.

Two highway men were talking. One was having marriage problems. He said the signs were all there. The other man suggested that he didn't read them right.

My husband doesn't just walk away from a fight, he limps away.

A fisherman married a large woman. He said she was the biggest catch.

Two couples were invited over to another couple's house for a dinner. After dinner they talked about reality tv shows. The host husband said you might not believe it, but my wife was in a reality tv show. They asked which one. The host said no I want you to look at her and think what show she might have been on. Finally one husband ventured "It wasn't America's Worst cook show was it" His wife whispered that she hoped she wasn't a winner. It  became quiet and you could say the dinner party was over with no more invitations coming again.

# A Lightning Bolt of Laughter

A stockbroker said his wife was only doing marginally better than he was.

In rice country they throw rice at weddings. In corn country they throw popcorn

If clothes make the man than my husband is a bum.

Girl was getting ready to drive and was reading the rules in the book to her divorced mother.
Don't leave the scene of an accident.
Mother asks are they taking about cars or marriage?

My wife keep complaining that she needs a change in scenery. So I went to a picture store and bought a large picture of a beach scene to take the place of our mountain picture we have hanging in our living room.

A wife was talking to another wife about her husband. He had hit his head very hard. He didn't have a concussion, but the last there weeks he has been acting strange. When he talks he makes sense. The other lady said "Well someone needed to knock some sense into him."

I didn't know until I retired what a planner my wife is. She daily plans things that she wants me to do every day.

A math teacher gets married. She has finally found the right number.

Rumors are that the chicken farmer is henpecked by his wife.

So after watching the movie I asked my husband what he thought about it. He said he couldn't believe the bad haircut the hero had gotten. They had the whole movie to fix his haircut. That's my husband always a barber.

Her marriage was not a good one. She was married to a comedian. When someone asked why she stayed with him, she said he amuses me.

A man said his wife is bright and sunny. After thinking about it he said well maybe just sunny.

It isn't good for a stock broker to get married, if he is going to keep his options open.

An artist was asked how he found his wife. He said it was drawn to her.

Some people get married and tie the knot, but unfortunately the knot isn't tight enough and the marriage falls apart.

In the country the man was calling "Sugar." The other man asked him if he was calling the horse or his wife.

I was selling my joke books at a grocery store. One couple came up. The man looked like he had too many prunes. He had a sour look on him. I told the wife I can see you are going to need to get one of my jokes books.

The woman went to see a psycic who told her she would finally find her true love. The problem is that she has been married for over twenty years.

Only in Spain the woman was asked where her husband was and she said he out fighting some bull.

Her husband a UFO fan was always testing his outer limits.

A bread man says you don't want your marriage to go stale. When your wife wants to freshen up, you need to let her.

The older man was standing around looking rather lost at the mall. A security guard asked if he needed any help. He said he lost his wife. The guard said I can have her paged. Oh please don't I want to enjoy the peace and quiet while I can.

It is all about getting even. A man stole another man's wife. To get even the other man stole the man's dog. He said so far I think I have the best deal. The dog keeps me much better company than my wife ever did.

Sanitation worker said that he an his wife have a disposable income.

Two different baker's children were getting married. The younger girl of the bride was the flour girl. She carried a bag of flour down the aisle and sprinkled a little on everyone. People expected that at a baker's wedding. Downstairs the green dishes were from one bakery while the red sides were from the other one. There was some competition to see which ones people would choose. Of course there are two wedding cakes. One from each bakery. The one man looking at all this and the cakes said "If this don't take the cake."

It was the Friday night card game. The one man was telling how much he loved owning his own business and being his own boss. He bragged that nobody told him what to do anymore. You guys ought to try it, its great. About ten minutes later the one guy came in from the kitchen. He told the bragger that was your wife on the phone she wants you home now. Well I fold I better be on my way.

The wedding cake for rice farmers is always a rice cake.

My husband is a runner, but he says he won't run the extra mile for me.

I complained to my Indian father that my husband and I had lost our house. He thought for a moment and said so what's the problem you still have that tent I gave you don't you.

Wife to husband after his mother shows up unexpectedly playing to stay awhile, I just knew it was going to be trouble when my horoscope said that was trouble on the horizon for me.

A lady said her husband couldn't go his separate way. He would be lost if I didn't map out his life.

One wife mentioned to another wife that her husband was turning seventy. The other wife said that is the same age as my husband. I always thought your husband looked so much older.

Being married to a math teacher isn't easy for the husband. Just when he has her figured out and comes with some new problems.

The family doctor has known the family for years. The husband one time asked the doctor if he could suggest something to lessen the pain. The doctor thought for a moment and asked have you ever thought of leaving your wife?

My husband treats me like a baby. When we eat out he wants to spoon feed me. He has a sign on our car when I ride with him. It says "Baby on board."

My husband has a job jar. To make sure the jobs that need to get done are there, I have listed the same job several times. But I do have some fun jobs like take your wife out to a nice restaurant and surprise her.

My husband can be very childish and immature. He finally got a job at a daycare. If he behaves himself and does a good job he gets a gold star. It seems to be working.

The husband works at a zoo. Often he would be late in coming home. He just got so caught up in the monkey business at the zoo.

The gambling husband returns home. The wife does not want to hear how he loves her and how happy he is to be home. She wants to hear him say "All is not lost."

My husband is a recruiter. He is always trying to recruit others to help him.

Two couples were eating out together. The one lady asked the other one how her brother was doing, being she knew she had just seen him. "Oh he is keeping active and is well connected."
Her husband said to the other husband that means "He is still pulling scams and we think he is connected to the mob."

The company the couple had worked so hard to build up for the past twenty years had gone broke. They had many bills to pay, and that is why they are in bankruptcy court. The husband says to the wife, "We still have each other and our love." The wife says "I am out of here."

The lawyer in the bankruptcy court asked the owner's wife if she knew what had gone wrong with the company. She said that her husband and his brother are the brains behind the company. If you knew how lucky they are in that area, it is easier to understand why the company failed.

A couple was in bankruptcy court for the second time. They had the same lawyer both times. After the second time of gong broke, the man's wife run off with their lawyer because he had all their money.

Two ladies were talking. One said her husband has a soft spot. The other lady said your not talking about his brain again are you?

# Miscellaneous

Only vegetable grown that is famous in Belgium is the Brussel sprout. When you talk to someone from Belgium they often waffle on their answer

Tree talk One guy says he pines for the days when the trees were just branching out. The other guy says that is fir sure.

To dream about something that can't ever happen is to dream the impossible dream.

Advice from a bug man. When people are acting like flies and buzzing around you and keeping from getting anything done give them a good swat.

Deli worker in a fight. The other guy got a cold cut.

There were so many bugs in the old West. They had a itching post.

A worker asked up what is wrong with Bill he looks so down. He just found out he is on Santa's naughty list.

A tire man says he never tires of telling a good story. He tries to put a positive spin on his stories. So he doesn't tell the same story over he tries to retake the stories. When someone tries to tell their problem to the tire man, he usually says please spare me.

The furnace man says when he goes anywhere he usually packs heat.

Water companies always work from a flow chart.

A dollar and cents discussion
The way you do things doesn't make any cents.
You need to put your money where your mouth is, if you are going to see any
dollar sings.
If you don't change you won't make a dime.
The other guy says thanks for your two cents worth.

Many people just walk around with no idea of where they're walking. It is good
to walk with a purpose in mind.

When I feel like I need to be lifted up I ride the elevator to the top floor.

When they are working at the clock factory they are said to be on the clock.

A painter said when they don't listen to his clean jokes he tells off color jokes.

When a reader doesn't know something or how to do something,
they usually say they haven't read up on it yet.

We have support for our idea. Last I heard Edna said she is going to put all
her weight behind the idea, and if you know Edna she carries a lot of weight.

The favorite sport of vampires is bloodsports. When the vampire is late coming home he usually says he had to do some blood work.

A judge in a talent show says to the contestant that he really needs to have
some talent. The contestant said to the judge that after seeing his last two films
he doesn't think the judge has much talent either.

What part of your body do you use to get a ride? thumb

The best part of running the merry-go-around you get to tell people when to
get off.

Who says they huff and puff? Many a customer at a local tobacco store.

Shoes that lift you up are called elevator shoes.

The ghost hunter is always trying to get the ghost to give up the ghost.

Thunder is applause for a weatherman when he gets it right.

At the prison the teacher had those in his class come up with
a plan. Three of them came up with escape plans.

What part of your body often has a wild night while you are sleeping. Your hair.

Remembering Mary Eddie who had died
First lady she was brilliant.
Second lady Didn't she start up a company that after only a few years went
bankrupt?
Third lady she was smart.
Second lady asked didn't she marry two different guys who both ran around
on her?
First lady she was above average.
Second lady didn't she die broke?
Well I guess she wasn't all that.

If you lost something in the cave days, you would after to look under every
rock and stone to find it.

Some people have problems because they push when they should have pulled
or vice versa.

The lion didn't eat the skinny guy because there wasn't enough meat on his
bones. He didn't eat the other guy either because he didn't like white meat.

The undertaker said we need to listen more to others so we can help them. A lady died dead on her feet. Earlier she in the week she had told several people that her feet were killing her.

How did the pointer end up in the mental hospital? He reached his tipping point.

When you move from a first floor apartment to a third floor apartment, that is moving on up.

The bartender's name for his small child is half pint.

The pilot takes the skydivers to a dropping off point.

An undertaker says he knows where all the bodies and secrets are buried.

When a deaf guy is in trouble he signals for help.

When your not in the know, you end up getting all your information second handed.

A cook likes to stir up trouble. At other times she is cooking up a plot. I told the cook that I had a good idea. She said to put it on the back burner.

Sometimes seamstress can be so rude. They will say "Can I cut in?" Often when people act up they will tell them to snap out of it.

There was a feelings workshop. People were not sure how to act.
The leader told them to just feel their way around.

Robin Hood and his men were just outlaws until someone suggested that they band together. I am afraid there was a little bit of drinking going on. That is where the term the merry band comes in.

It was a very embarrassing time for superman. He was in the phone booth changing and a lady was knocking on the booth saying she had an emergency and needed to use the phone.

One time the Lone Ranger had taken his mask off to wash his face and a man looked at him and said "I know you, your my second cousin's son Oscar Livermore." Imagine the problem there would be if the Lone Ranger's real name was found out.

It is difficult when you score a zero on anything. That means we couldn't get anything right.

A man complained about the long day. He said if the day her been shorter he wouldn't have had time to make so many mistakes.

The prize given by the funeral home is a dead give away.

A tape that is named for a bird is duct tape.

An older man said he had so many empty spaces in his mind. These are the spaces he was going to put something, but he just can't remember what it was.

In Panama to celebrate bananas, they have a day where everyone goes bananas.

# A Lightning Bolt of Laughter

What term is named for pregnant women? A pregnant pause.

A man hadn't been to workout for some time. I asked what was wrong. He said he had a bad back. Did you see a doctor? No, it is just that so many people have been on my back about different things.

Someone wakes you in the middle of a dream. That is a dream interrupted.

A man was upset with his friend who worked for an investment company. He said I took your advice and lost lot of money. His friend said "Don't be upset with me. Remember I never said it was good advice."

A farmer thinking about the past says now in my hay days.

Along the New England coast instead of saying sure they say for shore.

A whistler that doesn't know what he doing is said to be just whistling in the dark.

The funeral home director said that the grave matter is finally laid to rest.

The bartender said his brother is a barrel of fun.

Sandwich named for a cave man is the club sandwich.

When someone says to you that something will grow on you. I don't know about you, but to me that sounds kind of creepy. What is the name of the most creepy plant? A creeping Jenny.

It can be difficult being so smart. Everyone wants to pick you brain.

A group of carpenters organized a splinter group.

When someone asks you if you are out of you mind. Do you have to pause and think about it?

I love to repeat myself at echo canyon.

A fireman was asked how he liked his food. He said it wasn't so hot.

Two guys were talking. One said what is in the past needs to stay in the past. We should forget and move on. The other guy says good try Joe but I am still going to remember that you owe me fifty dollars from three weeks ago.

It is difficult when you tell something to a writer. They always say wait a minute I want to write this down.

What's worse than an elevator that isn't working? One with you in it when it is not working.

When something happened a long time ago the astronomer says that was many moons ago.

Now days sleeping with the enemy is usually sleeping with someone from the opposite political party.

When someone says they don't know where to start you might suggest they start at the beginning.

He is like a straw man. He doesn't have a leg to stand on. He needs to be propped up.

The favorite nonalcoholic drink in Louisiana is gaiter aide. When the police in Louisiana get too busy they say they are swamped.

During the French Revolution people were happy if they could keep their heads.

A young man had his head hanging down. I asked if he was depressed. He said no. He had been doing so many brain teasers that his brain had grown so much that it was pulling his head down.

A man took his clock in to get it fixed. He told the man that his time is in your hands.

A bread man coming into a warm room says it feels kind of toasty here.

It is said that people from Idaho know how to butter up to people.

When things get bad we say ain't it a shame. When it gets worse we say it is a crying shame.

The gas man said you don't want to run out of gas to fuel your argument.

A dreamer's excuse was the best he could dream up.

There was no doubt in my mind. Others said you need to leave room for some doubt.

A seamstress with a drinking problem has been tying one on.

We want our clothes and shoes to have wiggle room.

What line most people want to be in is the receiving line.

Where you start isn't as important as where you end up.

In some places there are more bats than rats. That is where people when upset say "Oh bats."

A lady wondered about some things that had been going on around town. The deaf man said he hadn't heard a thing.

The old man is bent over. He said he should have listened when people told him not to get all worked up and bent out of shape

Man as nicknamed "One Way Max." Everything had to be his way or was no way.

A vampire is the first to say "Don't bite off more than you can chew."

When we say we more than we bargained for, does that mean we paid full price for the other things?

There is a fine line between working hard and hardly working.

The actor was caught in the act. Fortunately it was the third act so the play was almost over.

A tailor died. He was given a fitting tribute.

Uncle Frank died at the table when we were having a family gathering. I will always framer his last words "pass the gravy." To this day I get teary eyed when anyone says those words.

When superman ordered a drink or food he would tell them to supersize it.

Mind reader said she couldn't read the person's mind. You must have a closed mind.

A sheep farmer has some real strong fans. They are died in the wool fans.

A defeated egg farmer says he feels like an egg that has been beaten and whipped.

When a tire man tells a story he puts a spin on it.

In cave days when the prices were low we say they were at rock bottom.

Sorry to say that the sun is setting on the plans I had for the day that never got done.

It is your day to shine you have been scheduled to give the main speech at your local club. It is on a topic many should be interested in. You did research, wrote notes and rewrote notes. You practiced in front of the mirror. There so much too say you finally narrow your talk down to 45 minutes. You can't make it any shorter. The big day has arrived. The meeting starts quite late. There are longer discussions on some of the issues. A matter is brought up that wasn't even on the agenda. Finally the club president says go ahead Joe give your talk, just keep it to less than ten minutes.

An impatient demolition man says "Well blast it anyway."

A dancer has so many ideas dancing in her head.

The magic act was so bad that the only thing that disappeared was the audience.

At the campfire they were trying different things. One had put marshmallows on graham cracker. Another said I have a chocolate bar, Why don't we put that on it too? That was the invention of the s'more.

At a meeting the watchmaker's job is to read the minutes.

When one side of a farmer's family didn't turn out well, he said they were from a bad seed. When the farmer got disgusted, he said I hope I don't have to go over this ground again. A farmer cleaning out the barn hands a pitchfork to the hired man and tells him to pitch in.

A man was told he needed to change his image so he grew a mustache.

It is not easy for a big guy to have a squeaky voice. When he talks people ask him he is a man or a mouse.

When you are thrown into a world of darkness you can only wonder if you forgot to pay the electricity bill.

The answers are all filled away on my mind. When I can't find the answer I realize that I probably misfiled it.

A seamstress says it is okay to be taken in. She also tries to get her children to pattern their life after hers.

When someone has a smug look that means they think their right and you are an idiot.

Sign at bakery "Man does not live by bread alone so come in and enjoy some of our cakes."

If you are going to fly don't take off with a bad attitude. You need to have your mind up in the air.

The pictures of us that we really like are pictures that flatter us and make us look younger.

I was tempted to do the right thing, but than I thought nobody would believe I did it. I better just stick to my script.

Sometimes we all need a withdrawal from the love bank. Remember if you haven't deposited any love in the love bank you can't expect to get a withdrawal.

When they cry in Louisiana they are called crocodile tears.

If you don't learn to walk in a straight-line you will end up walking in circles.

A computer nerd wrote a book called "My laptop Experiences."

The master mind gets blamed for everything.

We usually eat food, but people will sometimes ask us what is eating us.

Most common pet name for an astronomer is Comet.

How can you lead from behind?

Two men were eating at a cafe. The one told the waitress that the food there reminded him of his Mother's cooking. The other man said I thought you told me your mother was a terrible cook.

The dairy farmer was telling the cheesiest story, but it was so full of holes.

A reader into dogs, dog ears the pages she reads.

Greeks can be quite into peace. They are often offering people the olive branch.

I feel like royalty today. I went to the dentist and he crowned me.

If the world is a stage than you must look for what part you are to play on the stage.

A grave digger saw a man putting his foot in the grave. He yelled at him "It isn't over until its over."

When someone says "The top of the morning to you", do they mean whey you get up, the beginning of the morning or near noon?

A lady was complaining that young people don't know their math anymore. They don't even know that twelve and twelve equal twenty.

One Indian tribe made a tentative agreement with another tribe. Because of the way they sat the Indians were first called squatters. If they were rich they were a two tent family. Every month they had to attend a pow wow meeting. This is when they might be reward with a feather for some achievement of have one taken away for something they did.

Don't knock knock knock jokes if you haven't tried them.

A guy broke up with a singer. She was just to high toned for him.

Randy has the gift of making everyone feel good. What does he say to make them feel good? Nothing special. He is quite rich so he just hands out money and everyone feels good.

A car dealer says he has more drive than most people.

An argument at a laundry over a pair of pants. One worker finally says "Just cut it short and hang it up."

A cleaner hates it when someone gives her a dirty look.

A dairy farmer says he is not afraid to moo when necessary. When people get in his way he says moo over.

A Chinese man said to his neighbor "You want to wok with me." He didn't know if he meant walk or cook.

Cheese is like bragging if you spread it on too thick people won't like it.

When we are wet most of us would like to be like dogs. We are told to go and dry off. The dogs get to shake it off and get everyone wet.

When a baker holds a party it is called a mixer. Everyone is told to mix it up and blend in.

When two candy companies merge it is a sweet deal.

An artist was asked to do something he thought was unethical.
He said this is where I draw the line.

When things go good for a sheep farmer it is by shear luck. Their favorite name for their daughter is Lampchops. Only a sheep man can ask his wife to be a lamb for him.

The flow we would all like to see more is a cash flow.

A card player said we need to learn how to play it straight.

The laundry worker was paid in folding money.

A boxer into candy started giving sucker punches.

A trucker says when he hears good news, it really takes load off his mind.

The manager of the wig shop was called the big wig.

The manager of the China shop said she wants to make herself crystal clear.

Many problems we have in life are because we step into them. We need to heed the warning to watch our step.

The water worker tells a man not to dampen his enthusiasm.

When a weather man comes into a lot of money it is called windfall.

One gardener complained to another gardener that he had a rough row to hoe.

A model had done well for himself in New York City. His face was on billboards, buses and in ads in magazines. He went home to visit his parents in a small town in Ohio. While there he was the past office to pick up their mail. A man was staring at him. He thought my fame has spread he recognizes me. He asked the man if he knew who he was. The man thought for a minute and than said "You sort of look like that man on the wanted poster that was up last week."

Fast moving people just jet around.

Guys who are close to their dog often name the dog Buddy. The dog is their best bud.

When a laundry worker gives a lecture she gets on her soap box.

There was a woman's luncheon. One lady got up from the table and walked away fast only to return a little while later. She said that was a relief it was over. One lady whispered to another and asked her what she meant. She meant she was glad she made it to the bathroom in time.

A woman tells a man that she has just talked to his sister. Do you know what shape she is in? A thought for a moment and than said I think she is round.

Postal workers have a party, it is called a stamping out party.

Pointers can be very impatient they often say will you just get to point.

A pilot tells another pilot he will meet him in the air. The pilot says he is dong good. He is reaching for new heights.

Now days there would be more war with the Indians. When they would offer someone the peace pipe, the person would say they were sorry but they don't smoke.

A daycare worker that became confused, was rattled.

Pastor says again I encourage you to take your problems to the Lord and quit bringing them to me.

After talking to a guy for awhile, I said you are one out of five. They say one out of five people have mental problems.

Bankers can be so boring all they want to talk about is dollars and cents. The banker tells people to remember to keep in check and balance.

The weather man suddenly left the tv station where he worked. They say he left under a cloud of suspicion.

If your just going to be on time than your never going to get ahead of time.

A pickpocket said some people are ripe for the picking.

The radio announcer always airs our grievances.

The chef's special are the leftover from yesterday that nobody ordered.

Two sky divers had a fight. You could say they had a falling out.

The ladies were preparing for the church potluck super. One lady asked if we could please not talk about dieting until we were through with the potluck.

Who said it is hard to find a mate? Someone who was trying to put socks together.

When a boxer tells a joke you have to wait for the punch line.

A cleaner wants a wrinkle free relationship. It is not going to happen. When we get older we all wrinkle anyway.

There was a problem in the church with what color to paint the parish hall. Both sides were getting quite upset about it and some were not even speaking to each other. The pastor finally said in life we must learn to get along and we can't have everything our way. You can meet once more tonight and if you can't agree on a color by tomorrow morning I am having it painted black.

A skydiver was asked if he had any advice. He said nothing really jumps out at him.

The bug guy is known as bugsby.

The captain of the ship said there will be lots of great food on board, so don't go overboard when you fill your plate. After all this is a ship.

The sanitation worker said "You won't believe some of the things that people try to dump on me."

A good book out there is titled "My struggle to get to the top." It is about a cleaner who used to clean on the first floor, and now after several years and a lot of dirty work she is now cleaning on the twelfth floor. This book is an inspiration to everyone.

How to say it backwards. Turn your back on them and say what you said before.

The cook said "I don't like what he said. It leaves a bad taste in my mouth.

When the colonists were upset with the British many a wife would offer them a cup of tea to calm them down. Unfortunately many others would drink and after awhile they couldn't remember why they were upset.

The book "My Life Underground" is a dark and dirty book about a miner.

The undertaker has written a book about things we need to be gravely concerned about like keeping up the graves and tombstones.

The color nobody wants to be caught with is that of red handed.

The plumber said his grandfather another plumber was the first one to say when going to the bathroom "I have to take a leak."

Two male friends were together.
The one man was complaining that his wife doesn't listen to him. He said now the kids are trained and they don't listen to him.

His relatives never listen to him. His boss never listens to his good ideas and even his coworkers don't listen to him. He finally paused. His friend said he had been thinking about something else and hadn't been listening.

A man tells the guest that he is like a worn out carpet. You have worn out your welcome here.

Gossip back in the cave days when two cave women were talking
Gal where did you get those stones? I would love to find some like that.
Did you know Jane got engaged? You should see the rock she got. You know she is the rock star in the family. Not so much her son, he is a stoner and just hangs out at rock concerts.
I don't know what is wrong with the father, he acts like he has got rocks instead of brains in his head.
I heard my neighbors are taking a vacation to a cave in the mountains.
I have been so busy the other day I lost something valuable and in looking for it I didn't leave any stone unturned.
I am hoping we can get time off and spend some time at a cave down by the water.

Life of the middle sister
Oldest sister was so beautiful. All the guys were lined up to take her out. She entered beauty contests. The problem was that later on they they found that beauty would only go so far and without many brains the marriages didn't last long. Now after thirty years of marriage the looks have faded. After several child births, she has gained weight and is now single. The youngest sister had so much talent, but unfortunately in the talent industry you don't often marry well and eventually more talented people take over. Now after three marriages she is divorced from her third husband and not working. The middle sister was stable with no real beauty or talent to distract her. She married the computer nerd who went on to discover some things that made them a lot of money. She had a good life. She raised three children and when her husband died he left her a very rich widow. Now after thirty years who do you think the men are calling on hoping to get a date?

He is in almost every picture. In many groups he stands in the background. Nobody knows his name but everyone refers to him as the dude in the background.

People say they have two left feet. How do they walk with two let feet?

Sometimes a farmer won't do something. He says it is against his grain.

A trail guide helps people to choose the right path for them in life. If they lose their path than they need to learn how to be a path finder.

Upset bug man is really ticked off.

It can be difficult keeping up with someone from the energy company. They just have so much energy.

A man is nicknamed the "Crusher." You will know why if he gives you a hug.

Taboid magazine gives out the mucky muck award every year. It is the award for throwing the most mud around.

It looked like a promising morning as I woke up. I even woke up before the alarm went off. I was think of all the things I wanted to get done today. I got tired thinking about it all. Before I knew it I went back to sleep for a couple of hours. That is what is known as a false start.

Many people are making blanket statement that cover everything that needs to be said.

Name of baker's cat is muffin and the dog is snicker doodle.

At a department store the clerk looked at another clerk and said you are sure dressing down.

Some people don't have many clothes on. We can tell them to get dressed but it is often to late to tell them to get decent.

A fisherman says to another fisherman if you can guess how many fish I caught in my bag I will give you both of them.

When a bug man is sick we say he has come down with a bug.

Most people don't care if things are one-sided as long they are on the same side.

In the small town there was only one hardware store. A customer noticed a man shopping with a mask on. He told the clerk about it. The clerk called the police. The man with the mask on said he didn't mean any harm. He had a problem with the owner two weeks ago and the owner told him not to show his face here again.

The mother is 85 a widow who lives alone in the family house. Her daughter calls her everyday to check on her. When she called one day her mother said she had a visitor stop by. He was a nice young man. The daughter said I will be right over. She came over all excited. Mother told her to calm down and to remember her blood pressure. But mom he was probably a con man who takes advantage of older people. Mother comments that she doesn't get much company. He stated for over an hour and I even made a light lunch for him. Please mom tell you didn't give him any money. Well he did share about something that if I bought it, it would be a wonderful aide for me. I said I couldn't pay for it in full so I gave him a downpayment of $3,000. Oh mom how could you? Now calm down I wrote the check out of a account that has been closed for years.

A fireman wrote a book called "Flames of Passion." Unfortunately it was so hot many bookstores refused to handle it.

A man was butting through the cemetery. The caretaker stopped him dead in his tracks.

Rice that is used for church meals is called glorified rice.

A cleaner said she wasn't drunk. That drink she had was just a drop in the bucket.

A place was selling dirt. The sign said "Dirt cheap."

Party favors are favors you can do for me at a party. A worker at the party shop said it is no party working here. The worker at the party show was asked to do something she thought was wrong, she said she would not be a party to that.

Canoe philosophy
Without a paddle you are only going to be drifting and not going anywhere.
Remember the canoe doesn't go by itself you have to do the hard paddling.
Be calm, you don't want to tip the canoe.
You can go as far as you have the strength to go.
Just remember no matter how far you go you have to come home.

Man of peace talking. What I am saying can be dove tailed in many places.

Lessons from the dishwasher
Need to start with a clean plate
Watch what you put on your plate
Don't overload your plate
Treat the plate with care it can break
We are all a little like cracked plates. We can be nutty at time but still we can be used.

A lumberman has yelled "timber" for the last time. A tree fell the wrong way and took his life. In remembering him several office buddies shared the sounds of his working. They stood apart and each said chop chop and chop. There was not a dry eye in the church. After that they buried him with his rusty axe.

# A Lightning Bolt of Laughter

When a banker doesn't like someone he calls them chum change.
The astronaut is finally over the moon and now is studying the sun.

When you get older it is probably not a good idea to get dressed in the dark if you want anything to match.

When a painter dreams they are always colorful dreams. At times he has nightmares when the colors clash or people have painted something the wrong color. These dreams are so real he often wakes up with paint on him.

The word "Yeti" was written on the back of a man's shirt. I asked what it meant. He said they are Italian. He has five daughters and their six child was a girl too. He said Yeti another girl. That is what they named her.

A puzzle maker says it is encouraging for most people when the pieces start to come together.

A woman told another woman that she was counting her calories. I stop when I get to 1,000. You don't eat anymore. No, I quit counting.

The undertaker has developed a dead pan look.

The reason why bus boys got their name is that in the early days they always rode the bus to work.

How different people like their food
The firemen like it burnt
Dairy farmer likes it creamy
The water worker likes it watery
The road worker likes it crunchy
The circus worker likes it over the top
The weather man likes it light and airy
The ice cream man likes it when it melts in your mouth

The ad at a pipe shop encourages you to buy their tobacco and put it in your pipe and smoke it.

So many cowboys died with their boots on. The local cemetery was called boot hill.

When someone left the malt shop in a hurry we say they left lickety split.

A small town to a whistler is just a whistle stop.

A shoplifter says to another shoplifter that she just needs a little pick me up.

An Indian man said he didn't understand another Indian man. He said he must march to the beat of a different drummer.

You would think someone would want to start, but most people say don't get me started.

A man saw another man struggling to get into his car. Being the good man he was he stopped to help. The man said he felt so foolish. After putting his packages into the car, he dropped the keys on the floor and locked the door, before he realized what had done. The brown van was full of packages. Fortunately I had a bent hanger which together we could work to get the van open. He was grateful. I went to find a parking spot. Later I heard about an incident at the mall where a family returned to their brown van only to find it locked and all their packages gone.

Ranchers like to see a bull market.

What number we call terrible, the terrible twos

Sometimes when you get off to the wrong start you just need to restart your day.

An artist choosing sides says the lines are drawn.
A positive person says he doesn't have any problems just lots of challenges.

The trip most older people take is a trip down memory lane.
What most people want to see other people do is change.

When someone knows some gossip about someone the usual response of the other person is to say "Do tell."

A local tribe in Africa is having a fund raiser. The chief is spearheading the event.

At the mall the man was selected to be in a taste test. After tasting it the man started to gag and choke. He quickly got a napkin and spit it out. He than drank a glass of water. So the tester asked what do you think of our product?

Bikers are not welcome in the auto zone.

A demolition man thinking about the good old days, says they are a blast from the past.

If he has so much head knowledge why do his feet get him into trouble and head him the wrong direction?

The news letter at the chicken farm is called "The Squack Box."

How does it work to put mind over matter? If I put my mind to it, it doesn't matter at all.

Some of us guys were just hanging out together. Tom my brother-in-law who works for the power company came by. He said "I can just feel the energy in this room." He was looking for some guys to help move furniture.

New book out "My checkered Past" is about a checkered cab driver.

A clockmaker likes to keep everything up to the minute.

I slept like a salad means I tossed and turned all night.

A dishwasher quitting says he is down to his last plate.

When a fireman tells a bad story it is called a smoke bomb.

Several women were working on a retreat. One was named London. Not everyone knew her. One worker asked where London was. One worker said I think it is in England.

A cook looking at this food says "Feast your eyes on this."

This animal has one of the worst images. It is the big bad wolf.

If a spider could talk to another spider he would ask what is on your web site.

People used to wear black when they were in mourning. I remember one lady wore black for three months when her loved one died. She must have really loved her husband. Oh it wasn't her husband that died but the cat.

# A Lightning Bolt of Laughter

The water man said that sometimes people are not in hot water, but just in a little bit of trouble. We say they are in lukewarm water.

For many when asked if they have made any progress they say they are not even at the starting gate.

Be careful for the lawn boy. He will mow you down.

Her cousin always wanted to be a model. How did that work out for him? He ended up in prison, but they say he is a model prisoner.

Some people have been acting like skunks lately. They have been raising a big stink about something or another. If you stay too close to them you will run the risk of smelling too.
When to many demolition guys get together there is always an explosion.

After awhile I got to know a painter and he started to show his true colors.

The only thing you must do when you go to a cleaner's party is to come clean.

A guy lived in a rough neighborhood. When he got confronted by some thugs he would tell them to back off he had a black belt and they usually left him alone. If they challenged him he took off his belt and started whipping them with it.

I was visiting a school with my deaf friend. A sign said we have to sign in. He told me that he already signed for us.

In what position must don't want to be caught in is the middle.

An actress was successful for years on stage, until somebody upstaged her.

You never wasn't to ask a family member "How dumb do you think I am?"

What is the most useful thing you can take to a desert island? a boat.

You can tell when someone is from Idaho. They say "See you later tater."

When we want to protect our family, we use the term from the Old West days and say we are going to circle the wagons. You can tell when a cowboy has been around his horse too much. You will say something and he will say "Whoa I just can't believe it." A cowboy is teaching his young child to ride. He tells him it is time to pony up. In the old West if they were traveling and there was just a bush or a tree that stop was called a quick stop.

Even if you lose you can always be dressed like a winner.

A lady was thinking so hard. I asked what she was doing. She said she was trying to center her thoughts.
Some people have a wild imagination. They need to learn how to tame it.

The older man was telling people that all the white hair he had on top of his head was snow on the roof. Another man said to his friend and watch out when he shakes his head the flakes fall.

When your older you find yourself doing everything in slow motion.

A pig farmer agreeing with someone says I want to piggyback on what you said.

What is the number one emergency everyone faces at least once? Where to find a bathroom.

I asked the seamstress how she was doing. She said sew sew.

An undertaker putting an expensive suit on a body says you are one lucky stiff.

A vet upset with a worker says don't be pussy footing around here.

He was a circuit rider with the rodeo. He didn't get to get in to many rodeos. You could say he was short circuited.

A gambler who is quitting says "Deal me out."
Every one but Grandpa hated his dog. They would go to see Grandpa and would be scared to get out of their car. The dog thought it was his responsibility to make sure nobody got into the house to see Grandpa. He would growl and snarl at everyone. Grandpa loved the dog, so they couldn't do anything about it. Finally Grandpa died. A few days later the will was read. One part said for whoever takes care of the dog I leave $100,000. Uncle Frank spoke up and said "I love that dog."

Have you seen the name of the eating place called "Wings and Things?" Image being asked what you ate and you said a thing.
The lady told the male baker that he had cute buns.

When there is a meeting at the television station the weather man is always concerned about the atmosphere in the room.

A clerk drops a package of cigarettes she was getting for a customer. She bends over to pick them up. I said I hate to see you picking up a bad habit.

A cook writes a mystery
The victim was carved up.
Each person looked at a slice of evidence
One suspect was getting upset and starting to boil over.
There was a chill in the room.
The plot started to thicken.
It was well done.
Hopefully justice will be served.

The woman asked her hair stylist what you would call her latest hair style. The stylist said a mistake.

A jeweler admitted in order to get more money he was the one who came up with the idea of putting rings on your toes.

Someone was sobbing loudly. Some one said oh for crying out loud.
A electrician left the small town to work in a big city. He was attracted to the bright lights of the city.

New word from the fruit grower is "pithy." Sometimes we feel pithy. We want a little bit of pity and feel a little down.

Most people after eating a Thanksgiving dinner identify with the turkey. They say they are stuffed.

Sisters don't get along. They are up in their seventies. They live up North. The one sister said that when she died she wanted to be buried in her fur coat. Her sister said "Where you are going you won't need a coat."

A tow truck driver talking to another tow driver who is in a contest says he will be pulling for him.

Two hair stylists having a conflict. You could say they were at cross hairs.

If you eat too much candy and other sugar products before you go to sleep you often have sweet dreams.

Man is tall and big. What is the one statement most people say to him? "You are blocking my view."

Now days often a close shave means getting your hair shaved.

When a card player finally deals, he always makes such a big deal out of it.

He is a renown artist, a very famous scam artist.

My brother-in-law is crazy. Lately I have been getting concerned that I have started to understand him.

Do carpenters ever get a hang nail?

What's worse than having no luck? Having bad luck. When we don't want to admit we aren't lucky we say we are just down on our luck.

A swimmer calls a place a dive.

A plumber calls it a joint.

The farmer says it is a seedy place.

The electrician refers to it as a dark place.

Two girl friends were meeting up with a friend of one of them at a lady's wrestling meet. They were in the hall waiting for the friend. A large lady came in with a mean look on her face. She looked like she could handle anyone. The one girl said she would hate to have to face her in the ring. The other noted her big muscles. This is probably going to be a good fight. Just than the friend showed up. She greet them and than looked up and pointed to that big lady. she waved at her to come over. She explained that her mom had decided to join them.

Rain man on a diet says I will just have a little sprinkle of that.

Sound man says just because I am your sound man, I don't want to be your sounding board when it comes to hearing your problems.

In the superman museum they have the original booth where he used to change clothes. They would ask superman how he was doing and he would say "Super."

A dairy farmer says people have been mooing too much.

Jason was a nice guy but had little ambition. His grades were poor, and he didn't have any goals. The only thing going for him was that he was a ladies man. Twenty years later I ran into him at a meeting. He was vice-president of a company. He drove a fancy car, lived in a big house and made a huge salary. I asked how he did it. He said he married the boss's daughter.

A Sunday school teacher trying to get her unruly students to behave says "Why don't we all try and act like angels."

The director tells the actor that he needs to play it down. Nobody needs to know what a big ego you have. Actresses go through various stages in life, but always want to be on the main state.
Nothing pointers like better than when there is an all points bulletin. Compliment a pointer by saying you have a few good points and your point is well taken.

Roofers are patient people remembering change comes one shingle at a time. The roofers have been working with Santa in writing a book called "My Rooftop experiences."

When something doesn't go right for the electrical he says it is a dark day.

My brother-in-law asked me if I wanted to come over and go out with him for some action. So I did. We ended up going to the dog races. I had forgotten how much he was into dogs.

At James's funeral everyone remembered the bright colored clothes he wore. People commented on what a colorful life he had.

When all is said and done who we really want the approval of is the loan officer.

The shop owner tells the customer to see what in store for you.

When you work at a dog kennel when you eat you find yourself chowing down.

A chicken farmer was the first one to come up with the game "chicken." When he got older he found himself going to bed with the chickens. The worker at the chicken farm has a rooster tail.

We all encouraged Joe to take a chance. He need to be strong and have some courage. So finally Joe did. When asked how he did I was told he fell flat on his face.

The miners say what happens underground stays underground. They don't dig up dirt on anyone. Remember some problems are only surface problems.

There is a role coming up in the local theater. I have a good chance of getting the part. So many girls have told me don't get fresh with me. The theater is looking for fresh talent.

It was during World War I when the first pin up girl was called a bombshell.

I was named in my Uncle Bills' will. Friend said I thought you two didn't get along. We didn't. What did the will say. Make sure that Tom doesn't get his hands on any of my money.

A clerk was talking to the manager of the bedding shop. He said "Go ahead and lay it on me."

A pointer always tries to point you in the right direction.

Sarah starts to say I have a good mind to, when someone interrupts her. Ruth says I have known you for too long and you have never had a good mind.

It was Halloween night. Two older teenager were dressed in all black and had on black masks. They were carrying some tools. With all the parties going they thought it would be a good night to break into some homes. Suddenly a police cruiser pulls up to them and shines the light on them. One turns around and says "Trick or treat."

The weather man said he learned to sing in a shower.

A man was kicking a package of cigarettes. I asked him why. He said he was trying to kick a bad habit.

Do you have any idea why people collect junk?

The first thing the bug people do when starting a business is to set up a web site.

What most people want to leave behind them is their bills.

It can hurt when you roll out of bed.

An old scorekeeper will be the one to say he has an old score to settle.

Someone is undressed and telling you some facts. These facts are known as the bare facts.

The swinging term we use is "I have to get back into the swing of things."

You have a horse but you really don't have a horse. What do you have" A Charley horse

I wasn't as rough as I looked. I just smelled rough.

When a nut grower sums up a story he says that is it in a nut shell.

When the book is cold they put a jacket on it.

Everything a guy did reminded him of food. He was lifting a barbell and he though of the bars that he had left on the kitchen counter.

When you are reading a mystery and the suspense is killing you, turn to the back and read the ending.

The vet tells the unhappy dog that the fix is on.

Now days if you hit many young men below the belt you would be hitting their knees.

Two member of a royal family get into a fight. We say they duke it out.

The man said he accomplished a lot at work. He couldn't find anything better to do so he did his work.

Mountain climbers often ask others if they have reached their peak.
The new project at the daycare is till in the infancy stage.

We no longer can call people stupid or dumb. We need to say they are mentally challenged.

A sheep reacher said he had trouble sleeping last night. He was counting sheep and one got away and he lost count and had to start all over again.

A young boy was moving his head around. He said his dad said he had to get his head on straight.

Someone who is always blowing bubbles it taking too many bubble baths.

Death notices
A firefighter he just went up in smoke.
A clock maker had an untimely death.
A librarian had been ill for a long time so her death was long over due.
The astronaut was brought back to earth.
The photographer reached the point where he was no longer in the picture.
The tire man's air had just gone out.
The book store owner had reached his final chapter before the end came.
It is okay if you die broke because you don't get to take anything with you anyway.

The photographer has some developing news.

There are those that wait out the action and those that want to get in on the action.

They asked the British guy why he didn't try something. He said it really wasn't his cup of tea.

# Music and Movies

Bankruptcy song
Where has all the money
Gone
Where has all the furniture
Gone
Where are all my dreams
Gone
Where is my happiness
Gone
Where are my friends
Gone
Where is my wife
Gone

Emergency songs for emergency workers
Rescue me
I am sending you a SOS
Old Beetle song Help I Need Somebody

When a music students sass we say they sound off.

Name of the new baseball song "Take it on home."

A music teacher tells a student to tone it down.

Wrestler's song "I got ahold of you and I won't let you go."

Sanitation worker's new song is called "My Wasted Years."

The song "I just have to be me" is hard to understand. Who else did you think you could be?

New songs by the Prison boys "Release Me" and "Help me find my way out."

A music teacher said people have problems in life because they haven't found the right rhythm.

Some bands can sound so brassy.

A music teacher is always hearing music in the air.

There is a new music group out by the shoe people called "The Loafers." They sing soul music. They have a well heeled audience. At the end they tie all their songs together.

Music group called "The Top Dog"
Songs
Walk like a dog
Don't be barking up my tree.
I love my fire hydrant
People are lapping up their music and having a howling good time.

The quartet was having problems with one of its members. He missed at times, was late and his sound a little off. He was a good friend and they didn't want to tell they couldn't use him anymore. Finally they decided to tell him they were going to be a trio so he wouldn't be needed.

New son by the firemen is "Catch on Fire."

A choir student told the director she was having a bad day. The director said she could tell by the way she was out of tune.

The new song "Moving on in" is a hit among unemployed guys who want to move in with their girlfriend.

New song out "Your Nobody until Your somebody."

In music class the students were all told to write a love song. One wrote a love song about how much he loved himself.

A music teacher is in trouble. She is told to go to the office and face the music.

The music group gets on stage and start to shake. Soon the audience is shaking too. They tell everyone to shake it up. The group is called the "Shakers." There theme song is "There is a whole lot of shaking going on."

A music teacher said he always feels upbeat.

Around Christmas time the male singer was singing the song "I still Believe in You." Boy asked his mother if he was talking about santa.

A pastor was thanking all the workers that helped with Bible school. He said he would sing their praises, but he wasn't that good a singer.

The best song of the clockmakers is "We have this Moment."

When the music teacher was sick she said she couldn't feel her good vibrations.

The choir director says when the choir agrees with her she asks for a chorus of amens.

She sings like a bird. Unfortunately it is like a crow.

The theme song of the workout club is "Let's Get Physical."

The famous song by the magician's is "Where has Our Love disappeared to."

The four friends were enjoying singing old songs thy all knew. One turned to Carl and asked if he would bless them. He said you want me to quit singing don't you?

The movie "All or Nothing" is just another movie about gambling.

The movie "Your Cheating Heart" is about a lady that was seeing two different heart doctors.

Seamstress movie was title "The Final Cut."

They need some raw talent for the part in the movie. The actor they hired was to play in a scene opposite a tiger. Now the tiger thought they raw talent looked like meat for the table and figured they were just bribing him to do a good job. Now raw talent is easier to find than a good lion. We can kind of guess how the scene ended up.

The movie "I can't hardly wait" is about excited children that can't hardly wait for Christmas.

The favorite movie requested at the prison is "The Great Escape."

Movie "That Darn Sock"
Famous lines from the movie
Don't pin it on me.
I am going to have to cut it short.
I feel so hemmed in.
I hope we can mend our heart.
I feel so tied up.
I need you to cut me loose.
The plot is starting to unravel.
Remember there is a common plot that ties it all together.
At the very end they tie up the loose ends.

"Flipping Out" a new movie about a man who has been flipping hamburgers too long.

A new movie out is called "The Man Who knew Nothing."
You would ask him what is gong on and he would say "Nothing Much."
There isn't a lot of talking by the man because he has nothing to say.
This should be a great movie for the many people who claim they know nothing.

New movie about firemen
It is called "Burn City"
There are lots of time when they play with fire.
You wonder if the hero is going to get burned in another relationship.
It is difficult to see the screen through all the smoke.
You hate to see his dreams all go up in smoke
Some famous lines in the movie
Do you have a match?
I love your smoky brown eyes.
You light my fire.
We can't eat there the sign says no smoking.
I knew it was love when I saw you in that smoke filled room.
I can see the fire in your eyes.
The movie is mad to ignite your passion.

"Once Bitten you will be hooked on love." It is just another vampire movie.

The movie "The Great Divide" is another math movie about a difficult division problem.

The movie "A Long Walk Home" has a lesson in it for young women. Don't have a fight with your date when you are a long ways from home and have to walk.

The new carpenter movie is called "I Saw."

I saw the return of the invisible man but I couldn't find him in the movie.

Spaghetti westerns are very popular in Italy. Everything goes better when you are eating spaghetti.

Movie about Mr. Clean
Scenes in the movie
First is one where the place is full of grime.
We find people caught in sticky situations.
There is unbelievable dirt in the movie.
There is even a scene where they throw mud at each other.
It seems there is no way out of this dirty situation.
Along comes Mr. Clean. He is the only one that can clean things up.

A carpenter can't understand the movie "A Bridge Too Far." Why couldn't they get the measurements right?

At the halftime of the scary movie they would turn the air conditioning down. Those in the movie felt the chills.

A girl asked another girl at a party why she told the guy who is close to ugly that he should be in pictures. Well you know they are making a lot of horror films this year.

My cousin tried out for a part in a movie playing a bad guy. He didn't get the part because he looked to bad. He asked if he could try again. They said nope too bad.

What night most people get a fever and they made a movie about it? "Saturday Night Fever."

It isn't easy breaking into Hollywood. My cousin Lisa was supposed to play a body. The first time the director looked at her face and said "Who put all the makeup on her and did her hair? She needs to wash it all off." The second time the directory yelled "Cut, her eyelid moved." Finally the director said just cover her head and show her feet. On her feet she had painted "Hi I am Lisa." Last I heard they were looking for a new body.

There is a scary movie out called simply "The Bug." People are scared because a bug is going around. The problem is that if you catch the bug you come down sick.

# Relationships

A electricity guy is in love. Every time he sees this girl he lights up.
He was so impressed with her because she was so bright.

A girl says to her boyfriend who is a mover that it is time for her to be moving on.

Sweet talk is when she says she is sweet on you.

Signs that a date is not going well
1.  Your date keeps looking at the time.
2.  They are nodding off while you are talking.
3.  You return from the bathroom and she is flirting with the guy at the next table.
4.  She keeps getting calls and says she has to take them.
5.  She keeps sneezing and says she is coming down with something.
6.  After you order your food she tells you how sick she got the last time she ate a similar order.
7.  Asks for a breath mint saying she has been having trouble with bad breath.
8.  Keeps seeing people she knows and says she has to go and talk to them.
9.  You run out of conservation and you just finished the appetizer.

A guy was trying to date a girl who worked at the morgue. She said this romance is dead on arrival.

The girl met her boyfriend who was a road worker, when he flagged her down.

A guy wore a shirt that says "I am a special catch."

A girl calls her girlfriend and tells her that some friends are getting together. She said she would bring the chips and asked her friend to bring the dip. Later when they were there, she said I looked all over and I can't find the dip you brought. Her friend said Bill is standing by the door.

I went with my girlfriend to a very scary mansion. It was around Halloween time and this was the place to go to. We went in holding hands. Suddenly in the first room we were in the lights went out and everything went black and something jumped out at us. I didn't plan to jump, but jump I did. After that she grabbed my hand and we headed for the next room. All the rooms were dark, with ghost floating and things coming at us. She squeezed my hand so tight. Finally we reached the exit and we were out. I looked over at her, but it wasn't her. I had been holding another girl's hand. The scary part was that my girlfriend came out, and was looking for me and saw us.

A young man was quietly having a drink at a bar.
An attractively came up to him and asked if he was a player.
He thought for a moment.
Well back in high school I played the trombone.
I can play the piano some.
Were you trying to get a band together?

A girl was interested in an emergency worker so she asked for his phone number. He gave it to her. The number is 911.

Some girls like the young corn farmer. He has such a husky voice.

A girl said her former boyfriend was a runner. She said she is not running around with him anymore.

A cook meeting her son's very skinny girlfriend has only one thing to say to him. She needs to get more meat on her bones.

A guy tells his former girlfriend who broke up with him that he sees her in his dreams. She told him that was okay because that is the only place he was going to see her.

The lady had been dating the heart doctor for over two years. It was Valentine's day and she was hoping he was going to ask her to marry him and give her a ring. She saw the little box he had and got excited. When she opened it, it was a key. He said it was a key to his heart. This after she had been pulling on his heart strings for the past two years.

Two laundromat workers were talking. The one lady said I feel like my life is stuck in dry nothing is ever happening in my life. The other gal said told her to consider herself lucky. My life has been spinning out of control for some time.

A security systems man said his daughter's latest boyfriend isn't even alert. He keeps telling me everything is okay and not to get all alarmed.

Best pickup line by a eye doctor. I have had my eye on you for sometime.

A girl has been dating a man from the post office who is involved in so many things that he doesn't have much time to spend with her. She wishes he would see her as priority mail.

A girl and her boyfriend were eating out at a special place. The first course was soup. She asked if they could change bowls. Later as they were eating he asked her why did she want to change when they were eating the same soup. She said her former boyfriend worked in the kitchen. He told her that if he ever saw her with another guy he would spit in her soup.

Two young women are best friends.
One says to the other you are my best friend.
The other one says yes we are friends for life.
The first one says I need to borrow $200 from you.

The other one thinks for a few minutes and says you know I don't really think we are that close.

The camera man is in trouble. When Ken is singing could you at least put the camera on him and get it off Lisa who I know you have a crush on.

A couple go to a romantic move. She picked it out. Right during the most romantic part when he should have been putting his arm around her, he is sleeping and snoring.

It was supposed to be a very romantic date. The date was down by the river. He was bringing a picnic basket for them and later he had arranged for them to go on a canoe ride on the river. Everything was okay until they were in the canoe. She said something which he didn't agree with, and he got excited and swayed the canoe and it tipped over. She didn't know he couldn't swim, so she had to rescue both of them. They were worn out and soaked. They had lost the canoe paddles. He turned to her and said maybe they should try this again. The moral of the lesson here is that if you want a second date don't tip the canoe over.

A girl tries her boyfriend like he is an idol. Her friend said I don't go for idol worship.

When it comes to asking girls out many young men have trouble with their opening lines.

A book said his girlfriend just didn't agree with him and she gave him indigestion.

Two guys were fighting over a girl. It didn't work out well for them.
She walked off with the boy who was watching the fight.

The guy at the metal hospital asked the girl what kind of nut are you?

The landscaper said his daughter's new boyfriend is the most down to earth guy he knows.

The guy has hazel nut eyes. He has chestnut hair. His face is shaped like an almond, and he has a peanut nose. The girls all go nuts for him.

My boyfriend was cuddled up with me on his sofa while we watched a movie. He said you are all that matters to me. You are all my world. His cell phone started ringing and ringing. He looked at it and said he had to answer it. A minute later he came back into the room and said it was his mother calling him. She needed him to do something for her right away. He says I got to go, see you later.

The lady had a bad complexion and trouble with her makeup. But not anymore. She is dating the funeral home director who is an expert at makeup.

It is hard to go out with a speech teacher who is already spoken for.

Boyfriend goes to girlfriend's house. She baked him cake to celebrate their first year together. He knew he was in trouble when he got there and she had made him a dump cake.

The two ladies were peeling onions in the kitchen of the restaurant. Both were crying. When the cook came in he asked them if they were crying over him again.

The tax man said to his girlfriend that she should stick with him if she wanted tax relief.

I go on a date to a very nice restaurant. After the dinner my date asks if I would like a desert. I told him no. I said I was stuffed and couldn't eat another bite. He says I hope you don't mind if I do, and he went ahead and order the most luscious looking desert. He ate every bite slowly saving the desert. I wanted to jump cross the table and eat the desert. Me and my big mouth.

A boy in the puppy stages of love follows a girl around everywhere. She says she doesn't know whether to pet him or kick him and tell him to get out of the way.

A boxer asks a gal if she wants to go a round with him.

A computer man tells his girl that he wants to download his love to her.

The calendar girl had a date but it didn't got well. She said he was just too outdated.

I broke up with a mover when he started to put the moves on me.

The ice cream manager has had so many girlfriends. It is like they are the flavor of the month.

A man notices a pretty girl by the elevator he is getting on. He asks her if she needs a lift up.

A young man is very interested in this girl and hopes to marry her some day. He is invited for dinner at there mother's house. This is his first meal there so he wants to careful and make a good first impression. Wouldn't you know it the mother fixed liver and onions. The one meal he hates. He said to himself I can do this. He cut the meat into small pieces put food around it and washed it down with water. He was sweating when he was done. At last I can enjoy the rest of my meal. The mother went into the kitchen and came out with another piece of liver and put it on his plate. She said it was the last one. Being you finished the other piece so fast I wanted you to enjoy another one. He thought I just know she hates me.

A girl says her boyfriend treats her like a door mat.
The other girl says it is time to take up the welcome mat.

A girl was going out with a guy who has been asking his money. She said if your going to waste your money, you could waste a little more on her.

The single gal's toilet wasn't working so she had to call a plumber. They had such a good time visiting while he was working on it. When it was ready to flush he had her put her hand on the handle and he put his hand on top of hers. It was love at first flush. Unfortunately after several months he broke up with her. For the longest time overtime she flushed the toilet she would think about him.

The guy had one of the toughest balancing acts I have ever seen.
Try to balance your time with three different girlfriends.

We both played the fiddle but my girlfriend was first chair. At times it was difficult playing second fiddle to her.

A cleaner broke up with her boyfriend. She found out that he had been keeping a dirty secret. He would put away his shoes dirty and sometimes there would even be mud on them. He would hide them in the closet so nobody cold find them. If he wouldn't come clean on this what other dirty secrets was he keeping?

There are so many fakes and guys who just want to take advantage of a girl. So they know the difference one guy wore a shirt that said "I am the Real Thing." A fisherman shirt says "I am a good Catch." The gambler's shirt says "Why not take a chance on me?" The butcher shirt says "I am a cut above the rest." The hunter's shirt says "I am the one you are hunting for."

A guy asked his roommate to play some notes on the piano while he tried to sing the notes. He had a date with a music teacher and wanted to get in tune.

The fireman told his girlfriend to go ahead and light his fire.

Frankenstein had trouble with his dates. Often they would say he creep them out, or they would call him a monster.

My girlfriend reminds me of a bird because she is walkways sending out tweets.

Two guys were talking. The one was upset that his girlfriend revealed too much of herself to him. The other guys asked was she taking off her clothes? No she revealed too much of her past.

A trail guide was happy that his girlfriend was following in his path.

A guy was running around in his apartment with just a pair of shorts on. His roommate said it is almost noon, don't you think you should put some clothes on? Didn't you say your girlfriend was coming over. He said yes, she said she would be her in a half an hour. But I don't need to get dressed. She said she wanted to see more of me.

A lady dumped her boyfriend after he told her that she was his main squeeze. She wanted to be his only one.

The jealous girlfriend was always accusing her boyfriend of having another woman in his life. Finally tired of the pressure he admitted there was someone else, his mother.

Girl to friend says she wants to date someone who is fun, exciting, treats me special and isn't afraid to spend money on me. The other girl said you need a reality check.

Guy from power plant is making a power play for her.

A girl says to a guy that she has feelings towards him. He said I have feeling towards you too. He thought "Unfortunately they are not good feelings."

A guy who used to date a certain girl wanted his friend who wanted to take her out. Be careful for the dog. Does he bite or snap at you? No but when the situation is getting romantic the dog always finds a way to pee on me. It sort of stops the romance right there.

The man worked at the mill. He said he wasn't satisfied with just any run of the mill girl.

A soft spoken fireman told his girlfriend that she may not see the fire on the outside but he promised there was fire underneath.

Finally the college senior had a date with the girl he wanted very much to impress. His roommate told him you can either dress cool or hot. He helped him pick out cool and hot clothes and lent him some of his. His roommate had to go to work. He said be sure and let him know how the date went when I get home. Later that night the roommate asked how the date went. He said she was over an hour late so my look was sweaty.

Ted was always bragging to his two friends how beautiful his new girlfriend is. He said heads turn to look at her. Finally his two friends got a chance to meet her. Afterwards one friend said to the other "I didn't realize Ted's eyesight was failing him."

Three gals were visiting a smaller city. They couldn't help but notice the good looking African American men at the beach. When a friend called one and asked how they were doing, she said we are enjoying the local color.

The young man had just entered the room at the party. Two girls were looking over at him and pointing. He could see them smile as they looked over at him. Sure enough they came over to him and walked right past him towards the guy who was standing behind him.

My girl friend asked if I wanted to come over for a fun night of play and fun. It turned out that we were baby sitting for three bratty nieces and a nephew.

My boyfriend got upset with my cat. He said there is more than one way to skin a cat. I had to dump him.

My mother likes it when I date a runner as long as he has a good track record.

# A Lightning Bolt of Laughter

A basketball payer liked a certain girl but she was out of bounds.

I liked to dance, but my boyfriend was a terrible dancer. He kept stepping on my feet and it hurt. I suggested they try line dancing.

My date asked if I wanted to go to a animal house. I thought he meant the zoo. I turned out to be his brother's fraternity house.

Two shoe sales clerks worked together and were dating. The girl said her boyfriend thinks he is a goody two shoes.

A librarian thought she could easily read her boyfriend. It turned out she was wrong about him. She felt she had misread him, and now had to offer him a second reading.

It was uncomfortable for the poor man dating the rich girl. He had been at there house and seen the dining table set, and he couldn't believe how much silverware was used. His girlfriend kept insisting the come for diner, and he kept putting it off. He didn't want to do the wrong thing when it came to manners, and he had no idea what all those forks were for. Finally he ran out of excuses and had to come. Imagine his surprise when they had a picnic lunch in the backyard and ate with their fingers.

Terms used by weather man in a dating situation
The date was
cold not very friendly
hot looked very good
fair she was just so so
windy she talked all the time
stormy they had a fight
foggy not thinking to clearly
misty she cried easily
sunny she had a sunny disposition

When the young man told the cleaner he doesn't mess around, she knew he was the right guy for her daughter.

Dating a girl in show business isn't easy. She always kept me waiting in the wings.

The romance wasn't going anywhere. They were both in their upper thirties and had been going out for two years. Her friend said it is time for you to put a little romance into the relationship.

She had her hair done, and was all dolled up. She had invited him over in the evening for a meal. He gets into the dining room and all the lights are out. There are candles on the table. "What haven't you paid your electricity bill? Gal I can't eat in the dark. I need to see what I am eating. I don't like surprises. Later there was a love seat and a comfortable chair facing the television. She motioned for him to sit with her on the love seat. She said her cat always sleeps on the chair. "Gal you can't spoil the cat. You need to show him who is the boss." He tips the chair over and the cat runs off while he sits in the chair. She says she feels a little cold. "Well I don't need this extra sweater." He takes it off and throws it at her. She has a love story on Hallmark. He looks at the time. "Hey it is eight o'clock time for the big game." He grabs the television turner and turns on the game. Soon he starts burping. He says that always happens when I drink too fast. She falls asleep on the love seat, and isn't sure when he let himself out.

A cook says her helper has no taste when it comes to men.

It is nice to date a gymnast. They do summer salts when they see you.

At the singles event when food is involved everyone is asked to bring something. Two of them are so cheap. One bring the toothpicks, and the other brings ice. Yes he even has an ice machine.

I know people think the lady is sweet, but it is really an act. She is only artificially sweet. She really isn't all that sweet.

A cook commenting on her daughter's boyfriend. She said he just leaves a bad taste in her mouth.

When a pilot likes his date he tells her that time flies when he is with her.

It is difficult dating a loan officer. There is always pay back time.

A girl complained that the guy stuck to her like glue. He was with her where ever she went. One day he wasn't with her. When a friend asked what happened, she said I guess we came unglued.

A guy asked another guy if he went by the play book when he asked the girl out. The book describes play by play what you should do. He said I did and than made a big play for her, but she still turned me down.

In spring when young people get looking all dopey, don't pay attention to what is being said and daydream all the time. They have been bit by the love bug.

A girl talking to another girl about her boyfriend. I don't know what he does but I think it has something to do with the military. He said he cleans tanks. It turns out he cleans sceptic tanks.

She tried to butter up to me, but I sensed she was fake. It was sort of like margarine pretending to be butter.

Date with a tire man. We ended up playing spin the wheel.

A date with a wolf man. We had a howling good time.

Date with a junkyard man. He took me back to his place. What a dump.

She liked to paint and considered herself an artist. He boyfriend said to wear her painting clothes because on their date they were gong to paint. They ended up painting his garage.

A girl wanted to go out with a guy who had lots of muscles. She needed him for heavy lifting.

A college junior is getting to be a pest of this friends. He can't get a second date with girls because he is cheap and dresses and acts like he is poor. In the meantime he wants to hang around his friends all the time and it is causing a problem for them. One of his friends decided to do something for him. He told a girl who tells everything that his friend is from a very rich family. They have more money than they know how to handle. He doesn't want anyone to know how rich he is because he wants them to like him for who he is. After that she told all the other girls about him and soon he was having many dates. Some of the girls didn't even seem to mind pitching in and helping with the expenses on a date.

A couple had been going out for several years. They were sitting together of the sofa holding hands. He told her to close her eyes and image what life would be like if they got married, and look at how it would be twenty years from now. When he opened his eyes, he found out that she had taken off in a hurry.

Who says you can count on me? Someone dating a math teacher who wants to score extra point with her.

I don't want to date the neighbor. He lives a little to close to home for me.

A good match she loved to cook and her boyfriend acted like he was starving.

The boyfriend had the shape of a pencil. His head even looked like a eraser. I asked if he was sharp. She said no he is dull. The problem is that when I go out with him I am always thinking that I should be writing something.

She had met his family so he later went to meet hers. He came back with bandages on. He said I don't think her cat and dog cared that much for me.

# A Lightning Bolt of Laughter

The girl was telling her two girlfriends that her new boyfriend was more than she ever hoped he would be. The one girl whispered to the other girl "Boy does she have low goals."

Her boyfriend makes deliveries. He just keep on delivering and that's what I like about him. Every gal likes to get packages.

A couple said they meet my accident. They were both involved in a car accident together.

A cleaner doesn't believe her boyfriend. She says you are just messing with me. One laundry worker was really hung up on another laundry worker.

My cousin was mixed up with the baker's daughter.

The lawyer said the judge was courting her.

# Saying

The light bulb company manager said we don't have too many bright bulbs working here.

When it comes to giving most say it is the least they can do.

Most people would like to be called a millionaire.

Someone who is very negative he is a naysayer.

A highway man says don't burn your bridges because you never know when you are gong to need to cross one.

What most people need in life is a wake up call.

People often say "You don't say."

We all die. We can either die healthy or happy.

How plump do you have to be to be pleasantly plump?

When someone is lazy you can only hope they will get all worked up. Many people suffer from lazyities.

A player will often ask someone else to play along with him.

When you act you want someone to say that you are a first class act.

For many you don't have to say anything. Your face says it all for you.

The only thing most men outgrow is their pants.

You throw someone a surprise party, and they say "Why am I not surprised?"

If you have to tell someone your important, you are probably not.

For many people the only thing that multiplies are bills and problems.

A lot of people want to step up but some should probably step down.

The seamstress often tells people to make it snappy. She is also the first one to pin up something.

What is often the hardest thing to do? Get started

What most people use to shed a little light on something is a flashlight.

If monkeys watched a show they would want to be in the peanut gallery.

When the fiddlier is upset he says fiddle de.

Drink a lot of coffee and you will be full of beans.

A farmer says he always has a field goal.

If not now, when?

What word usually comes after watch? out

If you are going todo anything in life go big. You can either be a big success or a a big failure.

The question of why is more difficult to answer than the question of who.

A fireman said the only thing we should burn is fat.

A electrician got married in a lighting ceremony.

An astronomer got married under the stars.

A trucker says he will discuss it further down the road.

People say "Say what." I don't know why we are supposed to say what.

A vampire says he wants a girl he can really sink his teeth into.

Who said we need to lead a balanced life? Your local tire man.

Many people in life just need to be pointed the right way.

Who first said "Make sure you close your barn door?" It had to be a farmer.

When a baker is surprised by what someone does he says "If that don't take the cake."

# A Lightning Bolt of Laughter

You never say things like "Over my dead body? to an undertaker.

Double talk I know your not at fault, but I still want to blame you.

Most famous line at the box shop is "Boy do I have a box for you."

When someone hits another person a ship we say they decked him.

I passed the art school with flying colors.

What we wish we were doing when we say we have reached our limit. fishing

Why do they call it a slumber party when nobody sleeps?

If you don't get your mind in gear your mind is going to roll backwards.

Who said "What a tangled mess?" Many a hairdresser

If you have a handicapped brain you are called a lamebrain.

If you want to get rid of a thought you say perish the thought.

Why do we tell people not to give it a second thought when most haven't given it a first thought.

If you wish for something and than change your mind you are said to be wishy washy.

What we need to lean from a trapper is when to keep our trap shut.

A farmer says we can't change some things they are just ingrained.

When someone says there are more fish to fry, you know they must be a good fisherman.

You don't want to say it is on the top of your head because it might just blow away.

Most pleasant drink is punch. Pleased as punch.

Who says I will lay it all out for you? Your local rug salesman.

The only size I want is a sizable income.

If I don't get the credit for anything, than I don't want the blame for everything.

It is a lonely place to be in a class by yourself.

We can't be right all the time but it would be nice to be right once in awhile.

When a wolf eats they often wolf it down.

A gentleman when he doesn't want to do something he just bows out.

Never tell a hunter that your game.

A hair dresser will give you body.

A mortician likes to think of his place as a body shop.

I can't remember if it is feed a cold and starve a fever or vice versa. I usually just end up feeding both of them.

Lots of people would like to enrich themselves.

The hunter says we need to offer him a sporting chance.

When people say you missed by a long way they usually say you missed by a mile.

# A Lightning Bolt of Laughter

The letter you don't want to be is a Zero.

Color of monster's eyes. He is a green eyed monster.

We would all like to thought of as the person with the big idea.

When people do something wrong they usually say "I don't know what I was thinking." They were probably not thinking at all.
The part of your body that cools in jail is your heels.

Looks can be deceiving so before you decide be sure and take a second look.

Happy meals are meals that someone else is paying for.

The landscaper started a grass roots movement.

I don't understand the expression "What works for you." Nothing works for me. I have to do all the work.

Often a clumsy person has shattered dreams.

Do you want people to be behind you and back you up, or do you want them to lead the way and you follow in their footsteps?

If you develop your laugh line it will help so you won't have a frown line.

So many people have trouble walking in a straight line.

Furnace man says lots of people take the heat for things they say.

I am not free but I can get you free. I am your local bail bonds man.

A magician says you never want to get to old to learn a new trick.

The best thing about being broke is that you can't lend money to anyone.

If you feel like a nail that means you have been taking a pounding all day.

If it is an unwritten rule how do you know to follow it.

How you are supposed to act on your birthday. Surprised

Dairy farmer says butter you than me.

The smartest part of the body is often the mouth.

All great minds think alike, Carl maybe you don't think like the rest of us.

We want people to see things our way.
Do we want to talk people into it or out of it?

Argument with our hands. On the one hand, but on the other hand. We ever wins this argument it will be hands down.

Would we rather solve our problem or just complain about it?

When people go to the library they say book me.

Many people have trouble with their brain flow. Things flow out, but not so much flows in.

What only your hairdresser knows is the original color of your hair.

Famous saying of a railroad man "Stop in Your Tracks."

When they say "I am only going to tell you this once" they are usually lying.

Hand talk when your talking to your hand.

Most people talk to other drivers who can't hear them while they are driving. The talk is usually not good.

Who said "The steaks are high?" Someone shopping at a local meat market.

Remember if you are going to get anywhere in life you will probably ruffle a few feathers.

Who said "I am between a rock and a hard place?" Many a man in the stone age. You would say it to if you had to pick rocks all day. But a man has got to earn a living.

The famous words of an art critic "Do you see what is wrong with this picture?"

When a ghost cries it is boowhoing.

Don't be flippant. That means always changing sides.

# Sports/Working Out

Who says "I call it the way I see it?" An umpire at a baseball game

A bowler tells another bowler if you are going to bowl you need to get your mind out of the gutter. A bowler said that when he bowls he likes to think of the pins as the pinheads he works with than bowls them over.

Wrestler says "I am gong to take you down."

What bird don't you want to be during hunting season? A sitting duck.

A swimmer can be a deep thinker. He has lots of ideas swimming around in his head. Some people don't get things because they don't let it sink in.

A relator was walking through the gym. He hadn't joined yet. He was just doing a walk through.

A baseball player tells the person talking to him to slow down. He says I can't catch everything your saying.

The baseball player had so many bad hits that he was beginning to develop a fowl mouth. A baseball player being asked something, says and on what do you base that on?

A new game out is called spitball. You spit on the ball real good and than throw it to the next player. You are not allowed to use gloves. They spit on and it and throw it to he next player. This is a game that really helps get the spit out.

If a wrestler doesn't succeed it is back to the mat. Sometimes we wrestle with our conscience. We need to let the conscience win.

The firemen's basketball teams called the "Hot Shots."

A man told me that he was entering the Iron man contest. There were going to be thousands entering it. He said he was positive he would place. He didn't look that strong or like he would be anywhere near able to make it near the top. I asked him how he could be sure he would place. He said someone has to come in last place.

When a baseball player is having mental problems we say he is way off base.

A runner was ill, but now he is up and running. The runner tells the other runner to get back. He doesn't like him breathing down his neck. How come if the race is neck and neck someone can win by a nose?

Swimmer says if you are going to get anywhere in life you need to wade out a little deeper. New workout by the pool boys. It is called doing the swim. You put your arms out ahead of your body and repeat it going around the gym. It is a dry swim where nobody gets wet.

What game was started by older people and played on cruise ships all over? shuffleboard

A depressed skier is always looking at the down side.

An older boxer tells a young boxer that he needs to be prepared to take a few lumps.

The difference between a light weight and a heavy weight has to do with how much weight their lifting.

Is a trainer getting too personal when they talk about your weight?"
Stretching classes help you reach the things that so far have been out of your reach.

A gymnast said when he heard something he really flipped out. One guy gives an opinion but he says there is a flip side to it also.

Ask a duck hunter how he is doing.
He usually says ducky.
When he gets dressed up fancy to go out he gets all ducked up.
His duck tails are hanging on his tux.

Three guys were duck hunting. Some ducks flew out. Two of them shot. One asked the third guy why he didn't shot. He said he liked to have his ducks all in a row.

A new swimmer just learning to swims said to be wet between the ears.

Two guys were working out on the floor. One reached over and touched the other guy's knee. I asked why. He said he had throbbing knees.

The nickname of the boxer nobody wants to fight is "Jawbreaker."
The boxer wears a raincoat when he boxes. He doesn't want the other guy's blood on him.

The last runner in a race is called the anchor man. Need to catch a runner before he runs off. The runner said with the little information I have I will have to run with it.

Do a hop, jump and skip. You are just a hop jump and a skip away from success.

Advice from a baseball player is to remember in life you have many more misses than hits but if you are gone got accomplish anything you need to take a few swings at something.

A man was struggling to be a mountain climber. When someone asked how he was gong, the other guy said not good. He hasn't even made it over a hill yet.

Unfortunately after a wild night patcher often throws a wild pitch.

A deer hunter refers to his son as a young buck. At time he tells him to get over things and just buck up. His favorite party is a stag party.

The workout place wants to help you reshape your body.

The baseball player tells the umpire not to count him out.

A man says he is a runner. He always runs a little behind. A runner always wants fast food and his car fixed in a rush.

A basketball player has an easy job. He says it is a slam dunk job.

A baseball player's son answers a question for the teacher. She says it is wrong. He asks if she could at least tell me if it is in the ballpark.

A guy was running around the gym with his arms out saying he was an airplane. The trainer stopped him and said he was grounded.

The lady put her hands up towards her chest and started trotting around the gym. The next lady started prancing around the gym.
A third lady would run and jump. She was definitely galloping. You could tell they were all into horses. Finally the manager told them all to quit their horsing around.

When a boxer leaves work he always punches out.

When you want to duck responsibility of being seen by the boss there is a new workout called "Duck." You are working out and the trainer yells "duck" and everyone ducks.

White Sox fans
They all have white socks and wave them at the other team.
They yell sock it to them.
Earlier there was a problem two guys got kicked out of the stands for wearing red socks.

My brother was hoping to make it big in baseball but it turned out that he just had too many strikes against him.

The new workout is from the malt shop. You start shaking at her head and move down your body. It is called a shake down.

Many times the boss will tell people to hop to it. The gym is offering a class to help you hop faster.

A trainer treats the new workers like babies. Before they can walk they have to learn to crawl. So she has them practicing crawling. Next he has them practicing baby steps. In the advance class he learns how to take big steps. On the stairs when he steps up and down you need to encourage him to take the step or someone will step ahead of him. Finally they are ready to step out into the world.

At the gym to decide who goes first, they say you go first you weigh more than I do.

The dog walk is another good one. You walk around bent over with your tongue hanging out.

A fitness club started a newsletter, but so many articles aren't fit to print.

Before they can work with ropes at the club they have to take a ropes course.

A guy was acting up at the gym. A lady said I got this, I am his trainer.

# Teachers/School

Student to teacher. I can't take anymore my mind is already full.

A college student says he is like his dad a trucker. They are both carrying a full load.

The longer the student stays in college two things get bigger. Their debt and their ego.

The mailman was so proud that his daughter lettered in track.

The science teacher kept talking about evolution to the class. Finally one student raised his hand and said "I see what your doing sir. You are trying to make monkeys out of us."

A college student who can't find his class is said not to have any class.

When the English teacher talks it can be kind of tense.

Teacher to student who works at burger king. I know what they say there but here you can't have it your way, but you have to have it my way.

I asked a math teacher what was wrong. She said she had a number of problems. A math teacher said you have to watch for all the add ons.

The geometry teacher told the student he was approaching the problem from the wrong angle. He said we will meet at the intersection. The math teacher asks the other person if he is square with him.

Teacher asks a student a question. Student says he doesn't want to be a know it all guy who has all the answers. I don't like to brag. Maybe you should give the other students a chance.

I told my college son that I didn't think he could make it in the real world. Now he wants to stay an extra year in college.

Professor hands back the seniors thesis. He said your paper can't be supported. It is full of holes. Frankly a lot of it is just plain rubbish. But because we share the same world view I can still give you an A.

A beautiful college teacher who has won several beauty contest was talking to her colleague about her class. It fills up fast with mostly boys. They all stare at me with dreamy looks, so I know I have their attention. The problem is that they don't seem to focus on what I am trying to teach them. It is just like they don't seem to mind if they fail my class and have to take it again.

The one thing besides money that a college student never wants to run out of is excuses for what he did or didn't do.

Teacher tells the students the way some of them act up in class they should be in the theater class.

The teacher having taught a lesson on emergencies and what to do or who to call in an emergency asked the students now who do you call in an emergency? One boy said his mother. She always knows what to do in an emergency.

A father was telling a man he didn't like the guy his daughter was dating. He is a real nut case and talks nonsense. The guy asked what he does. He is a professor at the local college.
College
I don't understand the teacher.
The teacher doesn't understand my paper.
My Dad doesn't understand my grade.

I was in a prime position to get a great grade. Image my surprise when the teacher sat me next to one of the smartest students.

The student missed several math problems. He explained to the teacher that he can't solve very problem. There needs to be some mysteries in life.

A teacher checked so many answers wrong with her red pen. Her friend said you must have had a red letter day.

A math teacher says if you want to get somewhere in life you need to quit running around in circles and make a straight line towards your goal. He says some students are circles ahead of other students.

The school where something funny is going on is a school for clowns.

The teacher asks the student what he is doing in his desk. He says he is looking for some answers.

This is not looking good for the math teacher's husband. She says she is right 95% of the time while he is right only 5% of the time.

The teacher said the problem in her class is that much of what she teaches goes over the head of the students instead of in their head.

Student says to philosophy professor that his philosophy is to be happy and carefree. Your giving tests and expecting us to learn something is interfering with my philosophy.

A college professor was giving a major test. The test would count for 20% of their grade. The student hadn't been doing well in his class so he knew he needed to study hard. He not only went over his notes, but those of a friends who took better notes. The morning of the test he felt quite confident that he could pass the test. The professor told them to clear off their desks. Then he told them to put their books on the desk. He said it was going to be an open book test. The only thing he hadn't done was to crack the cover of the book.

An English teacher says to students you know your subjects but you still have to learn your verbs.

When the college says the expenses are out of the pocket expenses, they usually mean out of your dad's pocket.

The professor from Idaho is known as Mr. Spudinsty.

A math teacher explains how important math is in an illustration. She says three men robbed a bank. When they went to divide the money up, they didn't know how to do it because they hadn't learned division.

Some teachers went into a room to work. The cleaner was there. They told him he should leave because it was going to get messy there.

The students in the fourth grade knew they were having a substitute teacher that day. They thought it would be fun to confuse her so they switched seats with boy switching with boys and girls with girls. The substitute could tell something was up with their giggles. She said she wanted to get to know them, so she was going to give them a test which was worth 20 points. Only they are not to put their names on the paper. When done with the test raise your hand, and I will pick up your paper and put the name on it that is on the seating chart. Suddenly their joke didn't seem funny at all.

Math teachers can be very calculating.

The weather had been quite cold. The teacher asked the boy a question, and he said he couldn't answer because his brain was frozen. He told her to ask later in the day when his brain has thawed.

The history teacher's past has caught up with him.

She is such a complicated math teacher nobody can figure her out.

The geometry teacher tells the student not to be obtuse with her. She says we have an acute problem.

The science teacher had an acid tongue.

# Work Situation

A guard that is working says "On guard." A guard never wants to be caught off guard.

The older worker was asked to show the bright new young worker the way things worked at the job. He explained everything to him. A few months later his coworker said he sure catches on fast. A few months later he was calling him boss. The lesson is that you shouldn't show or explain everything to the new worker but hold a few things back.

My boss is fair. He treats everyone badly.

The man from the lighting company always wanted someone to turn him on.

The lady at work has two small children. When a worker makes a mistake she will say "Someone made a boo boo."

Sign at door company says their doors close quietly so people won't slam the door on them.

When he worker at a packing company tells a story it is a packed story.

When two power companies are in competition it is a power struggle.

A man worked in a machine shop too long. It ready made him cranky.

A duty shop means that no one feels that it is their duty to wait on you.

She wanted to serve others. How did that work out for her? She is one of the best waitresses.

The undertaker tells his assistant to please quit calling this job a dead end job.

The sanitation worker says when something doesn't work for you, you may need to throw it to the curb.

Let me know if the boss is sending a better get busy signal.

The railroad man says many people are on the fast track. It is important to know your station in life so you know when to get off.

Hired man is complaining to the dairy farmer. The dairy farmer tells him not to go sour.

The undertaker's helper told him he had his work all laid out for him.

I asked the cleaner how she was doing. She said it was such a dusty day.

So people won't worry and get upset about things the boss often under states things.

Everyone at work, usually worked in teams or had a pal to work with but not Jack. He felt like he wasn't getting the attention he deserved. He took off a week so they would miss him. The problem was that he when he went back to work, nobody remembered that he had gone.

How come if we are told not to get personal, when we apply for a job we have to fill out personal information?

What shift do swingers work? They work the swing shift. They even have their own swing band.

The only thing worse than someone spreading gossip around the office is someone who is spreading germs around he office.

The boss upset with the workers tells them they can all be replaced. Well maybe not Hank our maintenance man.

He has worked to long for the vet. He says what is the otter choice?

The postman says you have to learn to address each situation differently.

A restaurant worker says most people are so full of themselves.

A trucker is a good person. They are always prepared to go the extra mile.

The way people get out of work is by saying it is not their department.

A tool man said you can accomplish almost anything in life with the right tools.

He works on a egg farm. His boss thinks his son is so smart he calls him an egghead. He says the rest of you your brains are scrambled. Advice from egg man. I am no egg pert but many people don't get anywhere in life because they don't eggcert themselves.

A boss tell his manager that what he is telling him he doesn't want the general public or the employees to know. The company is going through a merger and there is a good chance some of the workers will be laid off, and there may be a change in their job which they may not like. We don't want to panic anyone. Unfortunately the intercom was on and everyone heard the news. Panic time is here.

After a week on the job the worker thought this job is every thing I dreamed it would be and more. Now after three years at the same job the worker has nightmares about the job.

Two workers show up in the boss's office. One complains that Joe the other guy stole his idea. The boss asks how do I know that it is your idea and not Joe's? He said you know Joe he has never had a good idea yet.

Boss to workers says that he would like to thank them for working so hard on the project, but unfortunately no one worked that hard.

The workers were told to come up with a plan on what do do about a certain problem. One worker complained that the only plan he had was how to get out of work.

Application for a job at a animal hospital
My best friend is a dog.
I have been in the dog house often.
I like to run around at night like my cat.
I used to work for pest control so I know how to catch mice.
Some people say I am kind of catty.
I can identify with other animals.
Like the squirrels I am crazy about nuts.

It is difficult to run a pie shop when too many workers want a piece of the pie.

The boss went to a hug therapy class. Now every time at work when someone does something good he wants to reward them with a hug. A worker said he would rather get a raise.

What you don't want to hear from a worker at the Dairy Queen, "Were down to the last straw."

I don't know what it says about business, but the most important job in any small business is done in the morning and that is the job of making the coffee. If the workers don't get their coffee they will be crabby and be hard to work with.

The boss wakes up at night yelling and in a cold sweat. His wife asked what happened. He said he had a terrible nightmare where he gave his employees a big raise.

At work everyone wants to be in charge and boss others. A customer comes in who is upset and very angry and asks who is in charge. They all pointed to each other.

The car salesman said at time he really feels used. He says he feels like he has been devalued. Even his wife wants to trade him in.

When the manager at the ice cream shop is upset, he is reaching his melting point.

Things were shaken up at the malt shop. Advice from the manager learn to suck it up and enjoy the good taste. The worst thing a manager can say at a malt shop is that they are no great shakes. The belief at the malt shop is that everyone can use a little shaken up once in awhile.

Fireman talk What in blazes do you want? Can't you tell I am hot and bothered? I need to go hose down.

A laboratory worker says somethings have gone down the tubes.

A man bragging says that his work shows the type of man he is. Another worker commented by saying "sloppy."

The egg farmer is accused of playing shell games.

It was difficult for the young man. He worked in the fruit department of the grocery store hoping that one day he would be the top banana instead of always being the second banana.

An older vet talking to some young vets. Said you know there is a saying you can't teach an old dog new tricks. But most of you are just pups so I expect you to listen up.

Boss to employee who had just become a father says "I know you need you sleep but I prefer you don't sleep in the office.

The boss chewing out worker who got the procedure all work. Where did you learn to do this from anyway? The employee said from watching the manager.

The pharmacist says most people can use a dose of common sense.

A relator shows a lot. It is not a whole lot but it is still a lot.

The question all bosses ask when looking at their workers is does anyone really know what their doing?

He was the third one fired. When someone asked him what happened he said he was just in the line of fire.

A juicer came up with an idea on how to get your creative juices flowing.

The photographer's helper got in trouble. He looked at the very fat lady and said "We are going to have to get wider lenses here."

The committee at the car company was called the steering committee. Their slogan is they will work to put you in the driver's seat.

Several people were hired by a landscaper. He called them in to talk to them. He said around here you can call me boss. I don't want you planting your feet in my office too much. I want to see some real growth in you. I will know you have been working if you smell like dirt or flowers. After the spring season I can't keep you all, so I will be wedding some of you out.

My dad has been with the fire department for so long. They say he is high up on the ladder.

The boss told the worker to quit saying "A fat chance of that happening." We have a lot of overweight people working here.

A farmer thinking about the past says now in my hay days. A farmer picked up some teenage boys and gave them a field day on his farm.

At the employment office the worker was trying to find out if two guys had any marketing skills. Now he was just down to looking for any skills.

An operator said when she worked she felt like she was always on call. When asked how her day went she said she was on the phone all day.

The government worker tells the customer to be civil with him.

The investment company's slogan is "We can make you Happy."
Trust us with your money and you can be happy and not worry.
All the workers wear happy smiles.
They say we will treat your money with care so you can be happy too.
Only later I found out that the boss is nicknamed grumpy.
Doesn't there always have to be one grump in the group.

I asked the highway man what was his sign. He thought for a moment and said I guess the yield sign. If I yield it avoids arguments and conflicts. The stop sign is good too. It gets us to stop and think about where we are going.

Four men at work were assigned a project. They had a week to finish the project. One man was a little bossy and maybe a bit critical of the other workers. He really didn't think they knew what they were dong and voiced his concerns to them. On Tuesday night he told his wife that he didn't know what they would do if he wasn't the main one working on the project. The found out because on Wednesday morning he came down with the flu. He was sick the next three days and didn't get back to work until Monday. He figured they would still need his help with the project, but was surprised when one of the men said they finished it and had turned it in on Friday. He thought I better try to see the boss and tell him I didn't have anything to do with it. He was sure it was a flop. But the boss was busy and soon he was too so he forget all about it. At the end of the day everyone was called into the board room. The boss said I carefully looked over the project. I picked the right guys for it. I couldn't have done a better job myself. Congratulations. Don't you hate it when thing turn out this way?

A laundry worker says as she gets older she starts to fade. She isn't as bright as she once was.

A worker goes to see his boss.
He tells him how hard he works for the company.
If I don't get it right I keep on until I do.
Sometimes I even miss lunch when I am busy.
At time I stay after to work and often even take work home.
I hope you appreciate how much I do for you and the company.
The boss said he appreciated every worker. They are special to him. Now he says get back to work Bill.
The secretary hearing all this told the boss you made him feel worse. His name is Wayne.

When someone from the energy company feels excited about something we say he is energized.

Noise makers are those who when fired don't leave quietly but make a lot of noise.

The job doesn't fit him. He doesn't have much patience and he is a waiter.

When selling a dump relator calls it a fixer upper.

The term we use in the business world related to horse racing when we say we try to jockey for a position.

The guard was explaining to a new guard in training where all the cameras were at work. Cameras everywhere even in the halls.

He finally led him to a small room in the back of the building.
This is the only place there is no camera.
The room was much bigger than a closet but it held a cot.
He laid on it and said well good night.

An obnoxious worker said to his fellow workers that he had good news. One of them yelled your leaving and this is your last day here.

When a toilet flushes right we need to remember to thank a plumber.

Coffee maker is upset we say he is all ground up.

The boss said he always remembered the fun at the circus. The favorite part for him was when they would say bring on the clowns. He says I feel the same way when the workers show up.

The most loving place is the post office. People are always sending their love.

In real estate terms when a relater has been very sick and gets well he says I have a new lease on life.

The clock maker says we have no excuse for not knowing what time it is.

They say steel workers have nerves of steel.

When they hired the new gal she said not job was to big or to small that she couldn't handle it. Her first job was to clean the toilets. She wined "Do I have to? Can't you get someone else to do it?"

Joe would be happy and carefree. Than either his wife, children, relatives or boss would pull his strings than he would be down and sad. One day he was up and than he was down depending on whether they were pulling his string. His friends named him Yo Yo Joe.

I worked on a pig farm in Iowa. My boss was named Mr. Hog. When he got upset with someone he would call them a swine.
The only good things I learned was how to hog tie someone up.

Questions asked the water department
If they were hard someone answer the hard water questions.
If they were easy they answered the soft water questions.
The boss always filters any information he gives out.

The store manager told Karen to take down the sign "We love our customers." Michael has been giving everyone that comes in hugs and saying we love you.

A builder was upset with the contractor. He said his back was up against the wall. He told the contractor he couldn't use his building blocks anymore.

The dishwasher said the problem with most people is that they don't wash long enough so they shine. They need to have a glow about them.

A girl was being trained to be a cashier by another girl. The manager later asked how she did. The girl said she only made five mistakes. Did you correct her and give the right change back? No, because the mistakes were all in our favor.

An undertaker arguing with someone tells them they are dead wrong.

After the meeting was over the boss asked his secretary if she took notes. She said no one said anything note worthy. Well do it next time anyway. I am dully noted.

Working in a toy store
It is child's play.
To get along with some people you have to learn to play along with them.
Two can play the same game.

# A Lightning Bolt of Laughter

At times you need to go by the play book.

I tell people not to toy with me.

The museum had beautiful art and statues. I asked the guard what was the one question most people asked him. He answered right away saying "Where is the bathroom?"

A baker's helper coming to work says it feels like an oven in here.

I asked the cookie maker why she made those cookies. She said it was a snap decision.

In one afternoon at the company six different people are fired. That's what I call rapid firing.

A shoe salesman is struggling with a lady who is trying to get a into a shoe a size smaller than she normally wears. Finally he says this shoe horn can't work miracles.

Just for Halloween the clerks at the retail sore were told they could dress up in costumes. The winner would get a gift certificate. Martha won for her outfit dressed as a bag lady. The problem was that Martha had not entered the contest. It was what she normally wore to work.

When my boss at goodwill gets upset he loses all his goodwill.

A caretaker said so far at the cemetery no body is moving.

I have the most important job at the hotel. I give the wake up calls without which most couldn't carry on their business or life.

Sign at an automobile shop says "A good mechanic is hard to find. We should know we have been looking for one for years."

A painter said when he is up against a wall he paints it.

A secretary says her boss can't come to the phone right now. He is in an emergency meeting. The coffee maker broke and they are deciding on which one to get to replace it.

At the returns department a lady was bringing back a pair of slacks. The saleslady asked what is wrong with them? She said they are torn. The saleslady looked at them and said "Of course they are. These pants are a size sixteen and you probably wear a twenty."

When a reporter shows up to work he says he is reporting in.

The boss complains to his secretary that he feels he is not getting the respect he deserves. She thinks if he got what he deserves the workers would be throwing things at him

At the store I asked the young man what he does. He says I work here. The employees behind him heard the remark and started to laugh.

Question often asked the bartender is "What's on tap for tonight?"

A bee keeper tells his secretary to buzz the next person into his office.

The druggist said it is a tough job when you have to work with pills all day.

A note on the boss's calendar says be surprised for your birthday party. Every year his wife's tries to surprise him on his birthday. The secretary knows he hate surprise parties so she tells him about it. He writes it on the calendar so when the day comes he can act surprised.

The boss call his six manager into his office. He said he was going to tell them some news that was hush hush. They were not to tell it to anyone else. He said if you can't keep a secret you may as well go now. They all left.

The pilot was the first guy to land a job.

# A Lightning Bolt of Laughter

The undertaker's helper really gets into the spirit of things.

The boss asks for a volunteer to work on a project over the weekend. Sharon volunteers. He says we can't use you Sharon we are looking for competent workers.

The manager of the popcorn shop was popping mad.

Our company has had to come up with so many plans to work things out. We are now down to plan M.

Oilmen working on hot pipes says they are pipping hot.

An advancement for a road worker is considered a bump up.

The first science fair
Comments on seeing Edison's light bulb.
Whose bright idea is this?
Hey bring it over here we could use some light here.
A man with an accent said and Watt is this?
And of course the famous line "How do you shut off the light?"

Who said it is in the bag? A local sacker at the grocery store.

A guy from the mattress company says he hates when people spring something on him.

Boss said he taught his workers to work together in teams. Now they have all teamed up against me.

My uncle has been making people smile for years. He is a photographer.

You can imagine how discouraging it would be to be a door salesman. All you do all day is show people the door.

I asked the guy from the can factory to do something for me. He said no can do.

The laboratory scientist had to run into the lab in a pouring rain. He works and experiments with mice and rats. His assistant looked at him and said you look like a drowned rat.

A gossip columnist says her job is messy. When she knows something the coworkers always tell her to spill it.

A hairdresser to another hairdresser about a story she was told says I don't know it just doesn't gel with me.

A baker tells his helper not to mix him up.

When a photographer looks back at his life that is called flashback.

Boss tells employee that he is the least productive employee. He doesn't get much right. He is not a good team member and is slow on the job. Tells him that he is going to have to let him got, but says don't take it personally.

A boss talks to a worker in his office and tells him he has to try and get along with his coworkers. He said I haven't said anything bad to them. I know but your shirt says it all. The shirt says "I work with a bunch of morons."

Games at work
Tag- You are told to do something, but than you touch someone else than they have to do it, unless they touch someone else.
Hide or seek Your manager is trying to find you and you are trying to hide from him.
Tattletale I see Joe playing games on his computer. Susan has taken her fifth personal call from home. Ben is drawing funny faces on his paper instead of taking notes at the meeting.
The blame game is very common.

He works in a zoo. His jokes are so bad he has to tell them the hyenas to get a laugh.

The boss was very upset, so he called his seven employees into the conference room. The secretary had an envelope with some money in it on her desk. She went to the bathroom at three and when she came back at ten after three the envelope and the money were gone. The boss needed everyone to tell him what they were doing at that time. Two employees admitted they were in the break room having a snack and just goofing around. One said he had gone outside to have a smoke and another worker went with him to keep him company. A fifth worker said he doesn't do it often but he had to run a personal errand so he was gone at the time. The sixth admitted he was on the phone talking to a friend at the time. The seventh hated to admit but he was sleeping at his desk. You know the boss thought I was better off not knowing what my workers were doing. The money with the envelope was later found. It had fallen under the desk.

Saying at Rooms our Us store says we always have a room for you.

The boss asked a handyman if he could fix a problem they were having. He said "No problem." Later the boss noticed that the problem wasn't fixed. His secretary said "Well he didn't say he would fix the problem, just that he didn't want a problem."

A man is laughing while talking to his coworkers. His manager comes by so he turns his face to the other side and talks serious with him. He told his friend "I bet you didn't know I had a serious side."

A new man is working at a computer company. Everyone has a cubicle to work in. While working he hears a whistle. Soon he hears a whistle from a different spot. Later there is another whistle. He asks a guy what is going on. The guy says our motto is whistle if you need something.

There were some major problems at the weather station. It was said they were suffering a meltdown.

You were working in a shoe store, but now you are the manager. A fellow worker asks how does it feel to have your shoe on the other foot.

A boss comments on a worker by saying to the manager "I know he is serious about himself, now if he could just get serious about his job.

Notice put up at work
We are going to be evaluating your work performance this next week. That means we need to actually see you working.

A farmer says he has a growing problem.

A generous clock maker says take all the time you need.

Confession of many a worker is that they don't want to be the boss, but just boss others around.

Boss to former basketball player working for me. Tells him he has bounced around here for a long time, and now it is time for him to just bounce right out of here.

The vitamin shop was the first one to sponsor the iron man contest.

A electrician said not enough people remember to look at the bright side of things.

A heavy hired man worked on a pig farm. When he came into the house the son says here comes the porker now.

A positive plumber says he is going to plunge right in and solve your toilet problem.

The young man was interviewing for a position of working on a political campaign. He was asked about his experience. He said he had been lying since he was knee high. He had experience making up some very good stories, and went things didn't got right he could put a positive spin on the story. He was hired.

I asked the accountant if he was done. He said I would be if I didn't keep finding so many mistakes.

When a carpenter starts a new business, he hangs up his shingle.

The biggest ball handler of the year is the man responsible for dropping the ball on New Year's Eve.

When there was a worker's meeting there was one guy who always caused a lot of trouble. He would gripe complain and say things that got everyone upset. Also the meeting would drag on because he questioned everything. Finally some workers came up with an idea with the help of the manager. No meeting times were posted. He was given an errand to run that would take him out of the office and the rest of the staff quickly met with the manger for the meeting.

The man was interviewing for a job at the plant. He asked those interviewing him what the company does and what his job would involve. Afterwards he said he was confused and not sure he would want to work here. The interviewer said you described 80% of our employees.

They were investigating corruption at the company. Bruce at almost 300 pounds was their biggest target.

Joe at newspaper office finding information says he got the scoop. His last job was working in an ice cream shop.

The boss and manager commenting on a worker. He works so hard. He is always on time. He is very cooperative. He is easy to get along with. He has a nice personality. I just don't know if we can overlook the fact that he doesn't have a clue about he is doing most of the time.

The editor tells the reporter the article you wrote is not fit to print. It can not be verified. We cold be sued for libel. The reporter starts to leave. The editor tells him to wait. I have a friend who works for a tabbed magazine who would probably pay you big money for the article, and I am sure at least one television station would want it.

An accountant looking over the books says to the boss I think you can make a go of the company as long as you and your wife don't take any salary or money out for the next three years.

Secretary answer the phone She tells the wife her husband can't come to the phone because he is working on a big deal. Later the wife asks the husband about what he was working on. He said it was no big deal.

A dentist said he was having fun. He was just teething.

I guess I was a little sensitive that I was short. My tall boss was always talking down to me. Then the manager talked about my coming up to her level. I would get excited and she would tell me to take a short breath.

The body shop owner says "What's a body to do."

A postman says you should know how to address someone. At the job the boss wanted everyone to work together on a project. A worker asked if that was because the boss wanted to build team work. He said no it was because if something went wrong we could all share the blame.

I was quitting my job at the fun house. It seemed like all the fun had gone of it.

The boss tells the fired employee that we will remember his name but try hard to forget the job you have done here.

I usually get about three wake up calls a day. One when I get up in the morning, and the other two when I am sleeping at my desk.

The salesmen were at their weekly meeting. They thought they had been doing good. The chart shown that the sales were going downhill and fast. Finally one guy went up to the chart and told Joe you have the chart upside down.

A lady confronted another lady at work about a secret she had told her. She said "You promised never to tell and now it is all over the office." The other lady claimed she didn't say a word. Over hearing the conversation another gal asked how did the secret get out if you didn't tell anyone? She said that she might have written it down an left it on her desk.

A lady came to work complaining again that there was too much going on at home and work and she was afraid she was going to lose her mind. Everyone had heard her story over and over again. A co-worker said to another worker "I am afraid it has already happened."

The manager at the lighting company show the workers the power switch. When you switch it to on it is working. When it is switched to off it isn't. I need you workers to be on.

A retired operator gets all sentimental over her last call. She worked so many years that for a number of years after she retired she kept hearing a ringing in her ears. Finally it has gone away. Now she just hears a dial tone.

A cook said that sometimes his life is so bland. I don't know what seasoning to take to spice it up. What a cook feels that another cook has done something wrong he says that is in poor taste.

The woman at the information booth lost her job. They say she gave out to much information.

The manager was told to fire a worker at the machine shop. He went to tell him. He was in a room with other workers and the machines are making a lot of noise. He told him that he was sorry but he had to let him go. The guy couldn't hear. He said louder I have to let you go. Still the guy couldn't hear. He finally shouted you are fired. Six guys left work that day never to return.

Some tools were missing from the cement man's work site. He was asking his helpers if they knew where they were. He said he wanted some concrete answers.

I like it when we invite Jack to our parties because he is such a good mixer. He should be. He has been a bartender for years.

When people are on inner tubes on the river we say they are floating around. The same name applies for people who float from one job to another.

Unfortunately the only thing that was easy for the new worker was making mistakes.

The motto of the company is "We care about you."
A couple were discussing a financial plan with an advisor.
After getting the information he needed from them he went to see his boss.
He asked his boss what plan did he think he should offer them.
The boss said "I don't care."

I feel so alive. Maybe working at the funeral home isn't the best job for me.

The ditch digger says "You need to learn to get a handle on things "as he holds the shovel. It doesn't hurt to throw a little dirt on others. It makes others think they are working. You can't get too far in life without getting a little dirty.

The bedding store manager made a blanket statement that covered everything that needed to be said.

A swimmer who works in the loan office was the first one to come up with the idea of floating a loan.

Everything in the company works but the workers.

An impatient clock maker came up with the idea of a three minute warning. You wonder couldn't he wait a minute longer?
When the watch maker calls someone into his office they usually answer I will be there in a minute.

The car salesman always gets to say the last words which are deal or no deal.

News story being broadcast live from the cemetery. The caretaker hearing it said there isn't anything live here.

The box shop employees are excited their boss gave them a boxing day. Words have said in a box store "Do you want us to box that up for you?"

Party favors are favors you can do for me at a party.
Trouble at the party shop. A worker said it is no party working here.

A dishwasher says he likes things to be crystal clear before making a decision.

A ditch digger who is not going anywhere. We say he is all holed up. Ask about his job we say "How are your holes holding up?"

News for the clockmaker always has to be up to the minute. They had to let one worker go because he always did everything counter clock wise.

A gossip columnist says her job is messy. When she knows something the coworkers always tell her to spill it.

The power company has been working to empower some of its workers.

The workers at Hooters are so into gossip. You say something about someone and they say "Who Who."

A baker says remember when you are feeling whipped and beaten you are now ready to be iced.

Boss says to employee that he may have to let him go. He says you think big and this is a tiny tot shop.

Sign on shoe repair shop "Hobble over to our shop and we will fix your shoe." The undertaker's helper told him he had his work all laid out for him.

The photographer said lots of people are guilty of making a snap judgement.

Note in paper the obituary writer has departed.

The office manager said he would like to see more people get in the mood to do some work.

A guy from the mattress company says he hates when people spring something on him.

A carpenter tells another carpenter that his last comment was off the wall.

When there is a meeting at the television station the weather man is always concerned about the atmosphere in the room.
When small people are recognized the making of a movie. The director always says he would like to thank the small people who helped.

A baker's helper coming to work says it feels like an oven in here.

What doves are found at funeral homes. mourning doves.

He worked for a tabloid magazine. He was fired because he couldn't get the dirt on anyone. All he ever found was a little mud slinging.

Finally a company called "Guest Moving." When your guest have overstayed their welcome and you can't rid of them call guest moving.

I work in a dollar store where there are so many items. Now Bill who also works there and I are going together. You could say we are an item too.

One reporter when seeking a story is known as the bloodhound.
He knows how to sniff out a good story, and he can smell the trail that leads to the evidence.

The most exciting thing for a grounds keeper is when he gets to break new ground. I worked the night shift so long I developed shifty eyes.

John is such a hard worker, who seldom takes a break. He doesn't even like idle talk.

A young man has been working too long in the fruit department at Krogers. He wants to give all the pretty girls a squeeze.

Different reactions to do you work here. One said no, he just takes up space here. Another guy says no, he just has fun here.

A cleaner was bragging that he could out shine everyone else.

A railroad worker hates it when someone pulls the switch on him.

There were some major problems at the weather station. It was said they suffered a meltdown.

There was a new manager at the retail store. He was young and hoping to prove himself that he could handle the position. The store was a mess with so many things needing to be done. In less than a month he was told a team of four was coming to check out the store and see if everything was the way it should be. He panicked. He had one week to get the store ready. He worked every night, and paid other to work overtime. He just lived the store for the week. Finally he felt everything would be alright. On Friday the day the team was showing up a staff member went to see him. The secretary said "He is in his office crying. They called and said the team can't come until next Friday."

When I worked at the malt shop I always had to do the most work.
I would always end up picking the short straw. There is a lot of shaking going on at the malt shop.

There was a training workshop for future cleaners. They showed them different messes and than asked what they would use to clean them up. One said I would call my mom because she has been cleaning up my messes for years.

I don't know what to believe. I was told that the company was open and honest, but now I hear they have some trade secrets.

When a carpenter starts out they go from holding the ladder for someone, to climbing the ladder, and to finally being on top of the ladder.

In training the sales people the speaker says "I want you to take full advantage of ____" That is all many hear as they work to take advantage of others.

There was a drawing at the door plant I was one of the three lucky people who got picked to get a door. The first person picked number two which was a nice bonus. The second guy picked door number thee and got three days paid vacation. I picked door number one. I had to take the boss and his wife out to an expensive restaurant.

The key maker said all his jobs are key jobs.

# A Lightning Bolt of Laughter

It was a sad day for the clock maker. It looked like he would be facing time in the prison.

The photographer always says smile when you say that. Tells his helper while smiling "Your fired."

A potato farmer said there is so much going on in his brain that he feels like it is all mashed together.

A electrician said sometimes we have trouble because we are just focused on one thing. We need to look for more outlets.

The fruit grower wanted to start a company that would still promote fruit. He came up with the idea of fruit of the loom underwear.

A ditch digger was told to take this shovel and shovel it.

The oil man says "Well well well. "An oil man always wishes everyone a well. When things don't work out he just says oh well. Some things just don't sit well with him. He was given his own platform to talk on. They work with a well oiled group, but one guy doesn't fit in. He is crude.

A carpenter always wants to make sure the sides are even. He says he is inclined to believe the one guy over the other. He said the other guy has to many vices and hasn't been level with him.

The electrician says he always tries to stay positive.

The bartender says "Are you kegging me?"
Slogan at the belt shop "We want to help you buckle up."

I was remembering the good old days at the pig farm. We ate alot of slop.

The dance instructor says he will boogie on over.

Sign at mattress place put your problems to rest on one of our mattress.

We all had our plans, but than the boss came up with a master plan for all of us.

At the teddy bear company we are told to always be huggable.